Transforming the Cottage Industry

The Rise of Dental Support Organizations

Dr. Quinn Dufurrena

Table of Contents **Page**

Forward

Dental Support Organizations (DSOs) have grown in popularity and power because of the needs expressed by the community of dentists in both the United States and globally. *Transforming the Cottage Industry* will outline this growing need for change in the dental community, the adaptation of the DSO model to meet the changing times, and the concerns of the solo practice model. Also, it will address the misconceptions that all new models undergo. This book will also endeavor to look at the more human and sociological side of why we are at this crossroads in the first place, since change, no matter how timely or important, is always resisted. This book will address what makes change difficult and many times threatening to an old paradigm. We will look at the invaluable opportunity for those willing to adapt and shift.

Prologue

Strive not to be a success, but rather to be of value – Albert Einstein

Nearly 20 years ago, I first learned of the **Dental Support Organizations** model. At first, thinking beyond the traditional private practice was a tough sell; however, the DSOs financial benefits, administrative capabilities, and group structure resonated with me as a practicing dentist. I quickly realized the skyrocketing potential that the DSOs could provide the dental industry and the success that would be achieved for everyone involved. I knew instinctively it would be the future of patient-centered care. I was in.

For over three decades, I've practiced dentistry in many different arenas, from the military to private practices, to the nonprofit sector. What I've learned is that dentists and patients face the same issues almost everywhere. Millions of Americans still lack access to appropriate oral healthcare, and dental professionals are still unable to circumvent the financial and time limits that have restricted them for years. This combination has led to an ever increasing divided dental community in America making this a challenge that requires creative collaboration, clear education as to the true nature and opportunity with a DSO, and a strong commitment toward unity throughout the dental community.

It has become a mission of mine to help answer the many challenges dentists are facing in this changing economic and regulatory environment. My first step is to create awareness as to the advantages of the DSO model and bring to the forefront the concerns expressed by the solo practice model.

This means we must build on the **Association of Dental Support Organizations** (ADSO's) current code of ethics, identify data that will define and answer legitimate concerns, and offer innovative ideas to dentists around the country to help them collaborate with us as we tackle the issues facing dentistry, no matter the organizational structure. The discourse is complex and raises many questions that this book will illuminate as well as offer answers to frequently asked questions and inspire new thinking in a world of business which is creating new cutting-edge models.

The dental community is profoundly affected by larger healthcare concerns, since healthcare is one of the fastest growing costs for individuals, businesses, and government. The U.S. healthcare system is no longer sustainable. Woodrow Wilson said: "if you want to make enemies, try to change something." So, we will certainly make enemies within the dental community but when dealing with healthcare, we can no longer afford the status quo of any model of care that is inefficient. It is time to change the way we view oral healthcare and embrace all of its ramifications. As the healthcare community and the medical model change, they bring the same questions to the forefront for the dental industry, and these questions pit the solo practitioner model against the emergent group practice model or DSO-supported model. This division is not necessary. Unity is possible with an open mind.

Paradoxically, while physicians remain at the center of the U.S healthcare system and generate 80% of all healthcare spending through their orders, many physicians feel powerless to change the conditions that limit their professional effectiveness. In a dialogue on the future of medical practice sponsored by Sermo, the online physician community, one practitioner said:

"Private practice is doomed. I see few that are successful. The practices in my community that still exist are getting subsidies from the hospital (loan repayment guarantees, recruiting assistance), are supported by the feds (FQHC), or are engaged in what one participant so aptly describes as 'corrupt practices.' There are a couple of ethical, honest practices that are still trying to serve the public. But every time I see the docs in those practices they have bigger bags under their eyes and they look more and more tired and depressed. No young doctor wants to take any business responsibility or ownership position in a private practice anymore." Sermo, Feb. 7, 2012

It is time to change this debilitating trend by looking to the future from a broader societal view as to which trends are affecting dentistry today, so we can learn what we can from the transforming medical model.

What are the global trends we can study to implement a new model of healthcare and dentistry that will be both financially successful for every dentist and every physician while creating more real advantages for the patient? Primarily we, as a society, must address the hard issues of allocating resources for healthcare. It comes down to basic mathematics: Growth cannot be sustained. There are not enough financial resources, doctors, nurses, technology, or drugs to give every person everything they want in healthcare.

We must reallocate our resources to emphasize prevention and not chronic care. In dentistry we know that early diagnosis, preventive treatments, and early intervention can prevent most oral diseases that, when left untreated, have expensive and lasting health consequences. This book addresses these concerns, as well as the difficult question of: How can we better prepare for success in the new paradigm of DSO-supported dentistry? In the following pages, I will show the necessity of shifting from the role of isolated surgeon to team member, skilled in collaborative systems and leadership, and from an autocratic solo practitioner to a dynamic group leader and successful motivator. These shifts are at the heart of the DSO model.

Although we are talking about making a huge leap toward a new model of dentistry we are not alone in our transition. This shift is a global phenomenon that reverberates through the banking industry, our governing bodies, and throughout education, medicine, corporations and small business. Change from an autocratic model to a more relational and collaborative model of business is happening everywhere, and countless books are being written by doctors, psychologists, economists and socioeconomic gurus lending their perspective on the changes that are upon us. Discussing the reasons for this shift is at the top of the bestseller list.

I believe these trends are relevant and I will outline some of the top issues discussed by these authorities and share how they impact the changing model for dentistry. When we understand that there are powerful collective forces pushing for change, then we will more easily see why the new model is now up for serious consideration within dentistry and why those who cling to the old model of a solo practice, power, and control are finding their approach no longer sustainable.

In the *new order of dentistry,* that is based more on inter-professional relationships, we focus on the need to learn to lead teams while being an intricate part of that team. Entrepreneurial spirit combined with personal accountability will be the formula for successfully moving forward within the DSO-changing environment. As we peel away the layers of resistance and fear that permeates the discussion surrounding *practice ownership*, we come to the core that ultimately consists of individual accountability.

Now is the time to make difficult decisions. I believe whole-heartedly that we need to be the masters of change and not the victims of inaction. Who dares, wins.

I wanted to write this book to help people in the field of dentistry navigate the choppy waters of change and the "coming-of-age" pains that occur in our rapidly changing healthcare environment. I hope to open new windows of understanding to the opportunity at hand and to shed light on a global call for change while introducing some radical ideas that require new thinking in a field steeped in an old autocratic paradigm.

INTRODUCTION

"We generate fears while we sit. We overcome them by action. Fear is nature's way of warning us to get busy." – Dr. Henry Link

What is at the heart of this seeming divide in dentistry? The key to success for the dentist in this rapidly changing healthcare environment is to first recognize that the required change was brought about by a complex set of circumstances, which is outlined in the subsequent chapter.

Secondarily, to be successful going forward, the solution to this complexity lies in the basic human trait of *relationship dynamics*. In simple terms: Success is equal to being open to change and is directly proportionate to the quality of our relationships with each other, with our patients, and within ourselves. Yet, change is something most of us immediately resist, it is human nature and our quality of relationships in dentistry has waned due to the overwhelming needs of running a practice.

Change is not a threat, it's an opportunity." – Seth Godin

New Paradigm

Benign neglect is an attitude of ignoring a situation instead of assuming personal responsibility for managing or improving it. There is a growing commitment to quality of relationships in dentistry and the creation of a renewed freedom for the practitioner to practice quality patient care. Relationships have an essential relevance to the new

DSO model and the emerging focus on relationships is creating a new paradigm that is beckoning for change in the field of finance, medicine, and beyond.

What we are facing in the field of dentistry, and at the core of businesses around the world, centers on quality care of people, on our increased connection to patients and increasing the quality of life for those treating those patients. These basic human interactions were the cornerstone of a professional practice for those who pioneered dentistry.

Quality of connection and care was the currency that created strong private practices, but with the advent of technology, competition, and the world of insurance, these core connectors have been disintegrating. Instead of an attitude of ignoring this situation we need to assume personal responsibility for managing and improving our relationship currency.

The winds of change in dentistry point to a single ingredient on which recent business models do not usually focus on as they contemplate *"good business"* these days: Creating value by being trustworthy, caring, and having honest relationships, which we are now seeing as a singular priority in newer and emerging business models around the world. It is not a new idea really, but one we have lost and now need to remember. The quality of relationship between a skilled doctor and a fearful patient will always trump any other aspect of care. The relationships between dentists, physicians, psychologists, and psychiatrists and their patients have received philosophical, sociological, and literary attention since Hippocrates, and is the subject of more than 8,000 articles and books in current healthcare literature. As dentists, we need to protect this most sacred of doctor-patient relationships and not allow greed, control, or power to divert any of us from our much needed vocations. Nor should these relationships take a back seat to the rigorous day-to-day responsibilities of running a practice.

There are volumes written on the powerful healing alliance that is necessary between a doctor and his or her patients and how the fabric of this relationship is relevant to not only the successful healing of the patient, but also to the heart of the business and financial success. However, the balancing act between good clinical work and demanding business responsibilities for any solo dentist has eluded most practitioners. The DSO model endeavors to put balance back into the equation.

The marriage between these two concerns, patient care and business success, is pivotal to the DSO model. Relationships are a key to the success of dentists who want to create client retention, increased revenue, higher quality of care and an innovative practice.

The doctor-patient relationship has been and remains a keystone of dental care, in it data is gathered, diagnoses and treatment plans are made, compliance is accomplished, and ultimate healing occurs. Therefore, the most important aspect of the healthcare profession is this ever challenging, ever powerful, doctor–patient relationship. As you will see in the following pages, we are moving from what has been a *transactional* dental business model back to a rich and fertile *relational* model.

Yet, there are factors that threaten to change this essential relationship:

• The misperceived threat in the shift toward DSOs,

• The ever complex and changing insurance industry altering the dental landscape,

• The rising cost of technology, and

• The ongoing access to care dilemma

All of these issues strain a system already under pressure to adapt and be resilient, and they need to be addressed with care.

In the pages that follow, I hope to make every attempt to quiet the fears of those who hold onto the past way of doing things and hope to inject a fresh entrepreneurial spirit into a new generation of dentists, while acknowledging that they are, in fact, the future for dentistry.

In the second half of *Transforming the Cottage Industry,* I will focus on several major changes that have never before impacted dentistry in the ways they do today:

1. We have more women becoming dentists than ever before and they bring new ideas and desires as practitioners to their practice.
2. Dentists are graduating with higher debt and are unable to purchase practices from retiring dentists.
3. Established dentists are less able to sell their practices and retire.
4. Emerging dentists have a new set of values and desires for being a dentist.
5. Insurance companies are changing the game in a dozen different ways.
6. The consumer is more in control of their care than ever before.

I will address the difficult question of how better to prepare for success in the vibrant new paradigm of DSO-supported dentistry while protecting the essential fabric of the patient–doctor relationship. Increasing our quality of care in the work we do will help develop a new generation of dentists who are bringing to the forefront new values and personal goals as pioneering practitioners.

DSOs provide dentists with a source for practice administration and development resources, training, financing, as well as support with the ever-increasing liability and compliance requirements. DSOs help dentists reduce the amount of time, expense, and stress that goes hand in hand with the administrative responsibilities of their practices.

But, to start this dialogue between the solo practitioner and the DSO-supported practice, let's start with what the hell happened? Let's start with the *Big Picture* approach and see how we got to this crossroads in the first place.

Chapter 1

The Dental Tipping Point

A *tipping point* is the critical point in an evolving situation that leads to a new and irreversible development. The term is said to have originated from the field of epidemiology and represented when an infectious disease reaches a point beyond any ability to control it from spreading more widely. Now the term is more often used to note the moments in history that created unstoppable conflicts, disputes, resistances and fear because every tipping point necessitates large change.

A tipping point intends to illuminate the possibilities and the need for innovation and growth. They do not allow for going backward or for stasis. Not unlike Newton's First Law of Motion, a tipping point always continues in motion. When the only thing that can happen occurs, and the only solution to this is letting go of the old thinking and moving on becomes the obvious and only solution, a new direction evolves which changes everything, in time, for the better: However, not without first, the old system being thrown into dis-equilibrium. Dentistry and healthcare in general are at such a tipping point. There is no going back. But how we embrace the future will be a direct result of being open minded and possessing a willingness to let go of what no longer works.

An environmental example of a tipping point is Apo Island. This island in the Philippines introduced destructive fishing methods, which created a *negative tip*. These methods set the regional fishery on a forty-year downturn to near collapse. But, Apo Island escaped the collapse with a *positive tip* that included the creation of a small marine sanctuary, which then set in motion a cascading ecological and social change that rebuilt the fish stocks and returned the island's marine ecosystem to health. Japan had a similar experience with severe deforestation during the 17th century, which necessitated creating new sustainable forest management institutions in response to the crisis. Dentistry is simply another kind of system in need of innovation and a positive *tip*.

Malcolm Gladwell, in his bestselling book, *The Tipping Point*, reveals that any tipping point is that "magical moment when an idea, trend, or social behavior crosses a threshold, tips in a new direction, and spreads like wildfire." The DSO model is responding to the collapsing old model and is on the brink of spreading like wildfire on a worldwide scale.

Just as a single sick person can start an epidemic of the flu, so can a small and precisely targeted *push* cause a technology trend to take hold, the skyrocketing popularity of a new product going viral, or a drastic drop in the crime rate. Dentistry, like mainstream medicine, has reached this point and there is no turning back. Once the dis-equilibrium is under way a new balance will demand to be created. The DSO model is a response to this demand.

This needed discussion regarding the tipping point facing dentistry, will take us back to some of the roots that run deep in dentistry. It is time to challenge the long held beliefs of the solo practice model and how it can be enlivened and strengthened through the emerging DSO model. It is time to look to the future of dentistry with new and fresh eyes. Comparing the beliefs of the "old paradigm" to the new DSO model as it stands against the landscape of the already changing medical model, reveals that the nuts and bolts of needed change for any dental practice has tangible and quantifiable advantages and, as always, is accompanied by resistance and fear which is part of our human condition.

The goal of every DSO is to, in the end, free the doctor to pursue what dentistry is all about: Providing quality care for the patient instead of consuming time with paperwork, bookkeeping, and the daily grind of running a physical plant. This huge expenditure of time, when given back to the dentist, can be utilized for all the reasons he or she became a dentist in the first place.

A Dental Response to The Tipping Point

The excitement and the opportunity that comes with changing times, the new innovative questions that are springing up and the new breed of dentist emerging from dental schools are part of why this book needed to be written. Changing the focus from solo practice to the DSO-supported dentistry is only part of the change that is afoot. DSOs can in fact become a springboard for:

• A dentist's increased sense of contribution

• Increased revenue

• Valuable professional alliances and

• Personal freedom and quality of life

New Demands for the Dentist

Expanded dental teams are feeling a keen pressure to provide efficient, preventive, and quality restorative services. A new standard of care is being integrated within "patient-centered medical homes" in the medical world, but dental care services have not been as successfully integrated. With an increased demand for value by the consumer in their dental care spending, practices will now need to:

• Become more efficient
• Understand the substantial trend toward larger, multi-site practices as they continue to be driven by dental plan pressures
• Integrate new practice patterns and creatively address the increased competition for patients
• Adjust to the new healthcare reforms and Medicaid expansions, which now have a greater emphasis on expected outcomes and lower costs and

• Generate greater effectiveness, which will encourage alternative models of dental care.

The Group Practice

The DSO model supercharges one of the most powerful engines for success: The group practice. The power of community and the group is undisputed in business, psychology and biology and a key to unlocking the timeliness and the ethical business practices of the DSO model. Dentists are not the only ones facing the need to adapt. The entire healthcare system is in trouble and has begun to shift its orientation in the effort to adapt or die.

Medicine went through this tipping point about 10-15 years ago.

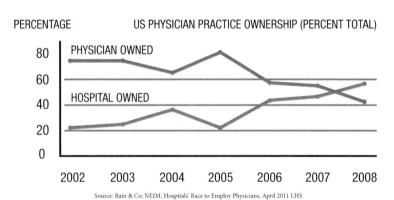

MDs JOINING GROUP PRACTICES

PERCENTAGE   US PHYSICIAN PRACTICE OWNERSHIP (PERCENT TOTAL)

Source: Bain & Co; NEJM, Hospitals' Race to Employ Physicians, April 2011 LHS

Chapter 2:

The Name of the Game

In the movie, Moneyball, Billy Beane, played by Brad Pitt, tells his lead scout "Adapt or Die" when he was confronted about taking a new approach to finding the best players for the Oakland A's baseball team. In real life, Billy was highly criticized as their general manager for attempting to defy the approach to scouting for talent that had been used for the whole of baseball, since the beginning of the sport. To say that the conversation didn't go well is an understatement, but in the end, with the new innovative approach involving statistical analysis called Sabermetrics, the Oakland A's made history and so did Billy Beane.

And there are well known examples of businesses who failed to adapt to their changing environments and in fact have either disappeared all together are in their last death throes: Blockbuster, Border Books, Seeds.com, American Motors Corporation who gave us the Gremlin and the Pacer and the U.S. Postal Service.
Adaptation is a change in which an organism becomes better suited to its environment. In adapting we have to let go of the attachments we have to the old ways in order for the new environment to flourish. Change management specialist, Torben Rick on his Blog *Meliorate*, lists the 12 reasons we all tend to resist change:

- Misunderstanding the need for change

- Fear of the unknown

- Lack of personal competence

- Attachment to the old way of doing things

- Low trust

- Thinking it is a temporary fad

- Not feeling consulted on the issues at hand

- Poor communication and misperceptions

- Changes to routines
- Exhaustion/Saturation/Burn Out
- Change in the status quo
- Benefits and rewards not seen to be adequate

These universal fears are why we hold on to our attachments to outdated ideas, to perceived power and control, and to personal beliefs. The tendency to hold on to the past is not unique to dentistry or healthcare and it will take a new kind of leadership to help navigate our need for change and address the resistance to these inevitabilities.

Many well-known authors write about *necessary leadership* during times of change, but few have lived it at the level of Lt. Gen. Rick Lynch. In his 2013 book, *Adapt or Die*, he says, "The world is in desperate need of authentic, reliable leaders at all levels of society.

Twenty-first-century leaders face unprecedented challenges and rapid change, and leaders with a keen ability to adapt are in high demand." At the core of his book is a call for embracing the principles of earned respect, working effectively with a diverse team, adapting to technology, and anchoring business on a foundation of trust, which is built upon personal and professional integrity. The DSO model intends to exemplify these needed principles of leadership, which are required during any period of change.

The birth of the DSO model started with one man who was willing to become an authentic leader against all odds and who was committed to a new and innovative model for dentistry.

A Question of Leadership: One Man's Story

"You are not here merely to make a living. You are here in order to enable the world to live more amply, with greater vision, with a finer spirit of hope and achievement. You are here to enrich the world, and you impoverish yourself if you forget the errand." Woodrow Wilson

Although there are numerous arguments that "size matters," great business models understand that it is not the size of your business that matters, but the scope of your vision. The DSO model started with the innovation of one man who earned trust, created effective teams, and for four decades has had the respect of the dental community.

Dr. Ed Meckler was one of the first dentists to see what might be possible for dentistry if he changed the solo practice model. But, changed to what and how? Not only did Dr. Meckler answer these questions, but also he created one of the most innovative and successful models for dentistry. He began his professional journey just like every other dentist: fresh out of school.

His risk taking for the past forty years has proven that innovation can be a powerful change agent and in his case, his dream for something different as a new dentist and his tenacity as a visionary changed the face of dental practices across the country and became the foundation for the DSO model.

Dr. Ed Meckler graduated in 1974 from Case Western Reserve University School of Dental Medicine and went immediately into private practice. He became a pioneer in developing one of the first innovative DSO models in the 1970's and founded Family Dental Center Service Company of America in 1981 to eventually become its sole shareholder in 1987. Dr. Meckler is now the Chairman of the Board of DentalOne Partner, Inc., a DSO providing comprehensive management services to full-service dental practices in 160 locations in 14 states and operating under the recognized names of Sears Dental, DentalWorks and DentalOne.

As an active member of organized dentistry and the founding Executive Director of ADSO (Association of Dental Support Organizations), Dr. Meckler has been an Ohio delegate and alternate delegate to the Ohio Dental Association. Dr. Meckler has been an Associate Professor at Case Western Reserve School of Dental Medicine for almost thirty years. He served as co-chair of the Ohio Dental Association Service

Company for eight years and has been deeply involved in the changing face of dentistry. Currently he is chairman of the Case Western Reserve School of Dental Medicine Capital Campaign and a board member of the visiting committee to the School of Dental Medicine. Dr. Meckler is also a Board Member to the Corporate Council of the American Dental Educators Association (ADEA).

In an exclusive interview, Dr. Meckler gave us the unprecedented history of how he pioneered the DSO model.

How did you get involved in the DSO business Dr. Meckler?

"I started out in private practice in 1974, and fortunately my practice took off very early. I found my practice schedule filled with several months of patients. For most dentists, with a busy schedule, it can feel claustrophobic because you are tied into your practice at every level, and it can leave you with no breathing room.

I wanted to find an avenue that would allow me some relief from my practice and still stay involved with dentistry. I started reading journals, (since there was no Google back then), and I came upon articles about Retail Dentistry. *Retail Dentistry* meant that a dental practice might be in a strip center or mall or in a creative retail environment. Well, I lived in Cleveland, which was the home of Sears optical and a light bulb went off.

I was fortunate to know the man who ran this endeavor, so I met with him and asked if he felt dentistry could be included in the Sears retail market just like optical, which had already proven to be successful. At this point, just five years out of school, I called Sears, reached a business executive and pitched the idea. His response was, "Why don't you put together a business plan?" Well, as a dentist I didn't know how to write a business plan, so I went to my attorney and my accountant and we worked together to come up with a business plan for opening a pilot dental office in a Sear's store.

I didn't hear anything from Sears for months. But, I was persistent and simply kept calling and they finally responded. They asked if I would come to Chicago and present my plan to their executives. I ran out and bought myself my first three-piece suit and a vinyl briefcase, jumped on a plane, and flew to Chicago. I made the presentation and then didn't hear from Sears for months. So, as always, I persisted and kept calling until I finally got a response from a fellow who said 'We really like the idea and we have an opportunity in Cleveland, Ohio, for you to open up a dental office and we will see where it goes.'

I took the leap and opened up my first dental office inside a Sear's retail store. I put everything on the line and went to the bank and signed my life away in 1981 to make this happen. Late in the 1970's, the law had changed, allowing professional practices to advertise. I felt my dental model in a Sear's location would be receptive to television advertising, so I went to a neighbor in the advertising business and put together a TV commercial with his agency. We called the ad: "The world's largest waiting room," and we gave our patients the whole Sears store so that when it was time for their appointment we paged them with beepers (devices that everyone had before cell phones). Also in the early 1980's, dental offices did not accept any of the few existing credit cards; but I worked with Sears so that our patients could use a Sear's card to charge their dentistry.

In the first year, due to advertising and the use of the Sears credit card, the office saw 22,000 new patients. After our first eight months, Sears called me and said, "Ed, we're looking at the numbers and the traffic in the store and we think it is a go." So they gave me another location, which did just as well. I had a model that was unconventional, in a retail environment, and using a completely different marketing approach and it had the potential of being a huge success.

I have to admit this was not my life's dream, but it felt that I was really onto something. So, I thought I should be opening up more offices. In the mid and late 80s, Sears was one of the powerhouses of retail with $60 billion in revenues and a diversified, growing portfolio, including

Caldwell Banker and Allstate Insurance Company. They also had a satisfaction guaranteed policy, so the alliance seemed important and mutually beneficial.

I followed my instinct and went back to my banks (even though I owed more than I could probably pay back), and I started opening more dental offices inside Sears locations. It got to the point that I had 38 humming offices that did quite well. I looked around and dentists and hygienists affiliated with me were successful, very happy, and I was growing equity. I woke up one morning thinking. "I have 38 offices now, with all my net worth tied up in these locations, how would I ever exit out of this?" The harsh truth was that there was not a sole dentist that I knew who could buy this group of practices.

The concept of this model was rooted in the idea that a business management model could make life easier for dentists. If someone would handle the accounting, marketing, supply purchasing, and all of the day-to-day business duties, the dentists would be able to focus on the dentistry and the dentists would be more efficient in their trained skills.

As your model grew, did you have any criticism or resistance from other dentists?

When I started there was a great deal of resistance from the dental community. I knew I needed to get into the various dental societies to explain the concept and to make sure I presented clear and detailed information. This was done in an effort to head off any myths. I was afraid that this new model would be thought of as competition to the solo practitioner.

I remember when we first opened an office in Chicago in 1984. We were not even there six months, and the Chicago Dental Society asked me to attend a society meeting to talk to them about what I was doing. I knew their early opinion of my model would be that it was competitive with the local dentists. And, I knew if I attended a society meeting to talk to them about what I was doing they would probably want to hang me. I needed to do something different, so I had a regional director go to the meeting in my place, hoping she would be a less likely target and that she could defer questions if they were too threatening. I am sorry to say they almost lynched my regional director. It was far rougher than I ever thought it would be. But, in this process of educating the dental community, Chicago learned that in fact this new model was not a threat at all and would open new doors in dentistry.

Our innovative marketing created more awareness, which created more opportunity for the dentists in Chicago and they eventually relaxed.

With 38 successful offices, I now wanted to grow the model faster. I did not have the capital for big growth, so I went to my lawyers and asked if I could sell equity in my practices to obtain capital to grow this model. They said a model had been proven in the optical industry, the pharmaceutical industry, and the medical industry whereby a nonprofessional entity would handle only the business end and allow the licensed professional to practice with his or her patients, focusing primarily on quality and patient care. I thought it was an interesting idea and was not aware of anyone in dentistry having ever tried it.

The biggest question was: What are the legal issues in this structure? The lawyers said that I needed to clarify the proposed duties of the non-dental support entity, and clarify what the clinical duties for the dentist would be, and then see how they would fit together. We met and created the structure for how this would work.

Once we had the new proposed model, it was clear that if we really wanted it to be official, we needed an Attorney General (AG) opinion to validate that the model could be executed legally. My legal advisors recommended that I talk to the AG. I let the AG know about the concept and told her that it would be nice if the office of the AG could issue an opinion stating that the model was legal. I attended many fundraising events, which gave me the opportunity to talk to the AG about the new model. In no time, I was able to get the first AG opinion on the corporate practice of dentistry. So, in 1995 it was determined that a "non-dental support company could affiliate with a dentist" with regard to the business side of a practice and not interfere with the clinical side of dentistry. It was a huge step.

Now, I was able to go to the private equity world with this powerful new opinion. I made my first private equity transaction collaboration with the private equity division of Key Corps Bank and Health Equity Partners. For the first time since that one pioneer practice in the Ohio Sears, I was able to pull out some equity for myself and finally get a pay check after all the years of building the model. The transaction also provided additional equity to support the growth of the supported practices from 38 to 90 offices.

The 90 offices were recapitalized a second time in 2007 with two new private equity groups: MSD Capital and North Peak Capital. I once again sold more of my equity at the recapitalization. Now we were off and running and grew from supporting 90 to 160 offices. The idea was that private equity could invest in a model that supported the nonclinical aspects of the dentist's practice. Their support gave the dentists the business acumen that most dentists did not have and offered cutting edge I.T. systems, marketing at highly professional levels, and analytics that they had never been seen. It also permitted the dentists to devote their time and attention to clinical, patient care. It was simply a win-win scenario.

That is how the model worked. And now I have been doing this for 40 years, and just this year I stepped down from being the executive director for the ADSO. Although I took a risk right from the beginning, it was the right decision, even when I didn't know what I was getting into. And I firmly believe it was absolutely the right thing for dentists.

What are some advantages of the DSO model?

The pluses of this DSO model are numerous. The DSO model offers opportunity for new dentists since the average graduating dentist owes, on average, nearly $250,000 in college loans with the cost of opening a new practice could range from $300,000 to $800,000. And older dentists are not retiring as early as they did in the past.

If a new dentist wants his or her own practice, the banks often don't want to lend money because of the graduating dentist's college debt and the high cost of opening a practice. So, in affiliating with a DSO they have the support of a thriving and powerful support model and they have greater freedom and quality of life, less debt, and the opportunity to make more money.

What do you think the future holds for the dental industry?

I am optimistic that the dental industry will come around and recognize that the DSO model is a better mousetrap. Traditional dental practices will always exist, and, at the same time, practices affiliating with DSOs will continue to grow.

What is currently the greatest hurdle for the DSO shift?

The issues are not about the patients or are the issues are about our industry leaders and perceived competition. Education is a huge part of what will make the difference. Dentists need to see how the DSO model operates and understand that it is not a threat. People do shift, and we are not going to eliminate all the people who are unhappy. Educating the dental community leaders and legislators is key. Those who are worried say we are "bad guys," and they have attempted to pass legislation to stop the model from moving forward. But in the end, I think there is no stopping this shift. Educating people along the way and meeting with legislators and lobbyists will get the story out there *correctly.*"

Adaptation

Progress is impossible without change, and those who cannot change their minds cannot change anything. - George Bernard Shaw

Adaptation is part of the human condition but usually only when change feels necessary. No one wakes up on a Saturday morning thinking to him or herself, "I think I need to adapt today." It always starts with a dilemma that the static answer no longer addresses. When the prevailing equilibrium is no longer holding and disequilibrium begins, the situation requires thinking outside the box. And for many, thinking outside the box does not come easily.

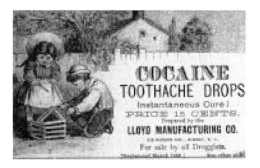

In 1885 this ad offered innovative help for dental pain and changed the face of dentistry from one vantage point. Yet, today this approach has been replaced by newer, more efficient, and technologically more advanced pain management practices. It is clear that dentists today would not hold onto this tried and true answer from 1885 simply because of an "if it works don't fix it" mentality. This applies equally as much to when a model for dental or medical care has outlived its apparent usefulness and needs to be upgraded to a model that reflects the current needs, desires, and changing face of the times with a new generation of dentists holding the reins.

Darwin's adaptation theory, also known as survival theory, is based upon a creature's ability to adapt to changes in its environment and to adjust accordingly over time. People resist adaptation when they perceive they will lose something. Adaptation is passed down from generation to generation until the whole culture adopts those changes to be better suited to their environment. Building on Darwin, what the prevailing business, relational, financial, and medical / dental models are experiencing relates to the concept of *memes*.

A meme is a behavior and idea or a collective style that spreads from one person to another within a certain culture. A meme acts as a "unit" for taking a cultural idea or practice and transmitting it from one mind to another through speech, gestures, writing or rituals.

Dentistry is in fact creating a new meme or, maybe more correctly, aligning with the new emerging memes of our culture. There is a tipping point in which a meme becomes the norm, the dominant idea, the new model, or the cultural system that represents the spectrum of healthcare.

Chapter 3:

The Changing Face of Healthcare and the Medical Model

Change is good. It's also often hard. But to succeed in business, you must run toward it. - Dave Kerpen

We can learn a lot from the changes happening within the healthcare system at large. Within the shifting medical model is an emergent giant of change: Complementary and alternative medicine (CAM) which can be defined as a group of medical, healthcare, and healing systems other than those included in mainstream healthcare in the United States. CAM includes evolving worldviews, integrative theories, new modalities, innovative products, and holistic practices associated with these systems used to treat illnesses and promote health and well-being by focusing on quality of care for the individual and strong doctor-patient relationships.

Despite their diversity, there are some common threads that run among many traditional systems of healthcare as well as systems that have emerged more recently. These similarities include an emphasis on:

- Whole systems
- Promotion of self-care
- Stimulation of self-healing processes
- Integration of mind and body
- Spiritual nature of illness and healing
- Prevention of illness

The current vehicle most often adopted to create the environment for this level of integrative care is more and more the *group practice model*. CAM practices are already adapting and adopting new patient centered and collaborative perspectives in response to the shifting paradigm.

The need to adapt is also running through mainstream medicine because solo practitioners face the same changes with the same set of questions as solo dentists. In 2013, Arielle Levine Becker wrote an article entitled, *Doctors Trading Independent Practices for Hospitals and Large Groups*, in the CT Mirror. In her article she interviews Dr. Douglas Gerard and she says,

Norman Rockwell prints hang on the walls of Dr. Douglas Gerard's office, and the New Hartford primary care doctor says his practice would fit into that era. Gerard is the only medical provider in the office, so he's the one who takes patients' vital signs and medical histories. His files are all on paper, and he's not planning to replace them with an electronic system because he thinks it will distract from the *face-to-face encounters* with patients. "It's a dinosaur, he said of his practice. Nobody's going to do this when I leave."

Historically, small independent medical practices have dominated the medical landscape. But increasingly, doctors are giving up their independence to join larger groups or hospital systems, often getting help with back-office functions, like billing and insurance negotiations, while staying in their old offices and seeing their same patients. And like Gerard, many people in the healthcare system think the days of independent, solo or small medical practices are numbered.

"If I had to predict ten years into the future, I think it will be very rare to find a practice that has no affiliation with a larger entity," said Dr. Robert Nordgren, CEO of Northeast Medical Group, a physician group affiliated with Yale-New Haven Health that has added more than 100 doctors to their system in 18 months. "It's a change brought on by demographics, technology and changes in the way healthcare is delivered and paid for, and part of a broader move toward consolidation in healthcare that includes mergers and affiliations among hospitals."

This is the future of medicine. This is also the future for dentistry.

As we have seen, the mainstream medical model has been feeling the reverberations of needed change for years and has stepped off the precipice to create new models for healthcare that support the group practice, providing us with substantial statistics to support that this was a hugely successful move.

Jerry Goldsmith, Ph.D., Associate Professor in Public Health Sciences at the University of Virginia wrote in his paper for the Physicians Foundation, *The Future of Medical Practices*, says:

From the solo 'micro-practice' to the patient-centered medical home practice, each holds the promise for diversifying physicians' service offerings and improving productivity. With the help of digital technology, which enables real-time claims management, payment, dictation, and coding, improving physicians' communication with each other and their patients, overhead costs are lowered and the practice is far more efficient.

As an alternative, many practices are coming together to form *practice-without-walls groups* or *super groups*. Some of these practices are single-specialty practices, coming together to achieve efficiencies inherent in scale, to reduce costs, and to create collective competitive advantages. Others operate more like independent physician associations (IPAs) due to the fact that they are multi-specialty practices.

So, what does a medical super-group actually do?

A *super-group* offers individual practices an opportunity to retain their individual autonomy and patient-centered care while reaping the numerous benefits inherent in being part of a larger organization. The primary purpose of a medical super-group is:

• Gain efficiencies of scale
• Centralize human resources
• Centralize accounts payable
• Contract and bill under a single tax identification number
• Negotiate better rates with insurance companies

By centralizing things like payroll, billing, accounts payable, and claims management, you can reduce the overhead that each practice has to lay out independently. More than that, a larger-scale operation reaps the benefit of lower collective costs for things like malpractice insurance, medical supplies, vaccines, and health information technology, and it provides the business resources best qualified to manage them. The DSO model is built on this successful transition that we are seeing in the healthcare community and its introduction of the group-practice model.

"With proper training and delegation, a healthcare team can see more patients, deliver better care, and feel more satisfied at work." – Peter Anderson, MD, and Marc D. Halley, MBA

Anderson and Halley go on to say:

A myriad of factors are challenging the financial viability of physician practices in general. Downward pressure on reimbursement combined with increasing costs have ratcheted up the pressure on doctors to see more patients each day just to stay even. The increasing administrative burden on doctors and their clinical staff has increased frustration and the potential for clinical errors and has reduced productivity and career satisfaction. None of this is new news, of course, the situation has been worsening for years. New ways to surmount the problems, however, are continually appearing. The *team-care approach* has improved professional satisfaction with practice, quality of care, documentation, and financial performance. It has increased patient visit volume while raising patient satisfaction.

The team-care approach is a win-win opportunity all around.

Like within the medical model, the new order of dentists are focused more on building relationships, protecting the quality of their personal life, and increasing their quality of care as a dentist, as well as creating a standard for success in business. This flies in the face of the autocratic, all-powerful approach that is inherent in the solo practice model and the old-guard mentality. Success now has new standards for excellence and is being driven by forward-thinking dentists with new values, many of them belonging to our new generation of dentists.

"The absolute fundamental aim is to make money out of satisfying customers." – John Egan

Entrepreneurial spirit, combined with personal accountability will be the success formula for moving forward within the DSO model. The result: Exciting and innovative possibilities, which will fuel a powerful future in dentistry and create a vibrant, lucrative, and creatively challenging environment within the dental industry.

Chapter 4:

Overview of the DSO Model

There is a real crisis in America due to multiple threats challenging the delivery of healthcare. Baby boomer dentists are reaching retirement age while at the same time there are regions of the country where needy populations still go underserved. Therefore, change is upon us in the dental industry, whether we like it or not, and questions like these need to be addressed:

- How can we learn from the new emerging models of patient care?
- How are the evolving clinical environments for dentists changing?
- How are dentists affected by the constant evolution of technology?
- How is the challenging economy for graduating dentists a game changer?
- How does this unexpected transition impact doctors in the latter stages of their careers?

These are some of the realities that are shifting the standards which have been adhered to for decades. These changes, and many more, have set the stage for this tipping point in our industry, and some innovative dentists saw this opportunity and this tipping point coming long ago.

After graduating from Southern Illinois University School of Dental Medicine in 1980, and starting his own office, Dr. Rick Workman knew there had to be a better way. He set out to create a world-class dental support organization to relieve the management burden for dentists by offering an array of nonclinical, administrative support, such as marketing, payroll, information technology, and human resources. By 1997, his vision to create this expansive support system for dentists became a reality.

Today, Heartland Dental, LLC, is one of the leading dental support organizations in the country, with over 625 - supported dental offices in 28 states. With more than 7,300 employees and 955 - supported dentists, Heartland Dental is currently the largest dental support organization in the United States.

Dr. Workman has received many awards, including the Ernst & Young Entrepreneur of the Year Award—Master Category, and is consistently featured as a guest speaker at trade events while also being the author of numerous articles in dental publications. In addition, Heartland Dental has been recognized in Inc. Magazine's Top 500 Fastest Growing Companies and has ranked sixth on their 2012 Hire Power list. Heartland Dental's mission is clear and their achievements show it: Every day they set out to support dentists and their teams as they deliver the highest quality dental care to the communities they serve while providing exceptional careers and creating value for their stakeholders. Dr. Workman explains:

Starting out with a handful of supported offices 18 years ago, it has been amazing to see how far this organization has evolved. This milestone is a testament to the hard work and the dedication of all Heartland Dental supported doctors and team members. They exemplify ideal leadership, openness, and passion. With the combined efforts of so many, we have become the largest dental support organization in the United States and continue to make strides in our mission of becoming the leader in dentistry.

Heartland Dental currently offers continuing education opportunities, leadership training, and nonclinical, administrative support, all contributing to continual growth and new inspiration for advancement. With that mindset, this groundbreaking DSO has supported hundreds of dentists and thousands of team members in discovering their ideal dental careers.

Heartland Dental was a pioneer as one of the first DSOs and is a current innovative model for dental care. Workman says:

The dental industry, as a whole, has not exactly embraced DSOs with open arms. Fearing the impact that new ideas and competition will have on their comfortable private practices has solo providers circling their wagons. Realizing that going toe-to-toe with the DSO model in a fight they can't win, they are taking the offensive by challenging the credibility of and attempting to regulate the DSO industry.

This leads us to ask: Why? Many of these objections and concerns that members of the dental industry put forward are ill-conceived and incorrect beliefs.

The DSO and the Group Practice

Transitioning from an isolated surgeon to a team member who is skilled in collaborative systems and leadership is imperative as we find ourselves in a consumer-driven industry.

Taking a leap away from an autocratic, solo practitioner to a dynamic group leader and motivator is exciting and accelerates quality of care, personal productivity, revenue, and the professional community. The benefits of making this shift are profound, and yet resistance still persists.

Some professionals, who resist the new trend toward group practice, believe that dental practices supported by DSOs are relinquishing clinical quality in favor of corporate interests who will violate laws and dilute professional standards. The DSO opponents are working overtime to make us think we must choose between profit-centered and patient-centered care. They want us to believe we will lose our rights to control the clinical side of our practice and that the corporately driven business side of the practice will cross over into the clinical side and dictate clinical protocol. These concerns are, in large, unfounded and untrue.

Major media has been receptive to this newsworthy claim, publishing articles and stories that fuel the fire against DSOs. Even political alliances have been marshaled to write legislation to regulate the DSO model out of the industry in an effort to hold back the sea of change. All signs, however, point to the exact opposite of these claims, which have been levied in an effort to cast a shadow of doubt on the emerging model.

Speaking of innovative models, we can learn a lot from Henry Ford, who set in motion a precedent for change and innovation, which lead, ultimately, to great profits as he changed the face of our society. Ford moved forward against a tide of naysayers. Ford's actions in the evolution and revolution of the automobile industry set a precedent for the change we want within our dental community.

In 1908, automakers thought the best way to maximize profits was to build a car for the rich. Henry Ford, however, had a different vision and wanted to produce a car that everyday people—like the workers in his factories—could afford. With lower prices, he figured that cars would be more affordable to the general public. He also decided that if he paid his factory workers a higher wage more of them would be able to afford the cars they helped make. Henry Ford would make a profit by selling MORE cars, changing the entire face of the automobile industry.

Due to his willingness to make necessary changes and innovative decisions against the prevailing winds of what other businesses said should or should not be done, Henry Ford's efforts to improve productivity changed the market for automobiles forever.

In October 1908, the first Model T Fords were sold for $950. As Henry Ford found new ways to reduce production costs, he passed the savings on to consumers at lower prices. By 1912, his cars were selling for $575. It was the first time that a new car had sold for less than the average wage of U.S. workers. The price of the Model T would continue to drop during its 19 years in production, at one point dipping as low as $280. With each price cut, more and more consumers could afford to buy the cars.

This reduction in price meant that the Ford Motor Company had smaller profit margins on each Model T, and revenue remained the same. How was that possible? In 1909 the profit on a car was $220. By 1914, the margin had dropped to $99. Yet, sales were exploding exponentially. While profit margins on individual cars were smaller, the added sales volume increased total profits. During this period, the company's net income grew from $3 million to $25 million. Its U.S. market share rose from 9.4%in 1908 to a remarkable 48% by 1914.

Henry Ford permanently transformed the auto industry. To remain competitive, other automakers had to mimic his innovations in mass production through the adoption of his assembly-line approach.

History is firmly on the side of the DSO model. New models of healthcare delivery have been loudly challenged by doctors only to be enthusiastically received by patients and ultimately prevail. Competition drives innovation and price containment in all industries. The DSO model creates competition and gives patients (the consumer) a real choice in their dental care and the freedom to more effectively utilize the benefits their employers provide as well.

The Federal Trade Commission (FTC) characterized efforts to slow the growth of DSOs in North Carolina as "anti-competitive." The FTC reported a study finding that corporate involvement in healthcare delivery actually "improves coverage and lowers costs." This is good news that certainly the editors of Bloomberg News and members of Congress might embrace. Once again, this is a story that needs to be told.

Chapter 5:

The Evolution Revolution

Evolutionary innovators approach a question because they see that there are limitations in the existing solutions. And as Jeff Stibel points out in his New York Times bestseller, *Breakpoint*, "Revolutionary innovators ask questions no one else has thought of."

Stibel notes that Robert Kennedy eloquently captured this sentiment, when he paraphrased a quote by George Bernard Shaw: 'Some people see things as they are and say why? I dream things that never were and say why not".

We have talked about how change requires adaptation, but before adaptation can occur, our dental community would learn a great deal from all that has been studied about how, as humans, we first resist change before we conform to the prevailing winds.

Harvard Professor, Robert Kegan, in his latest book *Immunity to Change* and in his earlier works *The Evolving Self* and *How the Way We Talk Can Change the Way We Work*, intended to help his professional readers overcome what he considers a predictable *immunity to change*. Kegan defines an immunity to change as our "processes of dynamic equilibrium, which, like an immune system, powerfully and mysteriously tends to keep things pretty much as they are." It is human nature to resist change when we value equilibrium and stasis.

It is also just as predictable that as any new model seeks to balance what is sorely out of balance, resistance will be the first line of defense because we are afraid of what is new and unknown. Yet, psychological, cognitive, and emotional developmental research has also provided us with a plethora of information on what motivates the human species to change at all. The answer? Disequilibrium and crisis are the motivators for change. Without a death, a divorce, a serious illness, or a perceived saber-toothed tiger, we would not change at all. Not one iota. The revolution of the dental industry is that mandate for change, and it will not be comfortable for many.

Thomas Climo is a Dental Practice Management Consultant and previously a professor of economics at the University of Kent, in England. He writes, "No one is shouting to stop the solo practice business model, a monopolist delivery system restricting both labor and ownership, to only a state-licensed dentist. In contrast, everyone, from solo practitioners, the ADA, and government committees and subcommittees, wishes to tear down the dental practice management (DPM) or the dental support organization (DSO) business model. The reason they give is that it is for the "benefit of the patient," and I know of no monopoly that has ever willingly given up its claim to the pricing and policies of the revenues it controls." This resistance is all about greed and it is all about fear of loss of control and perceived power.

"Power does not corrupt. Fear corrupts... perhaps the fear of a loss of power."
John Steinbeck

Climo goes on to say that, "A system that regards itself as perfect is functionally deluded. The strategy is usually to say the *monopoly* is in the best interest of the customer, a breakup would mean worse service and cracks in a system that is perfect. No mention is ever made of the monopoly assisting the monopolist in dictating pricing and policies and also creating an entry barrier that foils healthy competition, which would benefit the customer. It took eight years to break up Bell and AT&T from 1974 to 1982. Can you imagine what the price of a long-distance call would be today if this breakup never happened?"

"There are only two questions that human beings have ever fought over, all through history. How much do you love me? And who's in charge?" — Elizabeth Gilbert, Author of the best seller, Eat, Pray, Love

From a monopoly mind to a "hive mentality" is admittedly not an easy leap. Moving away from total control and toward shared responsibility and power feels threatening to many. It eludes the monopoly minded, who, in fact, as practitioners themselves, would hugely benefit from the very change they are resisting. In the long run, the truism, "that which you resist, persists and is made stronger" could not be any truer. The Model T in point.

Climo goes on to point out those "Who would compromise service to their customers in the mistaken belief that in doing so the bottom line would improve? That would be like Hershey taking away its chocolate and expecting people to still buy it as a chocolate bar. The moment your business, whether solo practice or DSO, begins to deliver a bad product or bad service, the days are not long before loss replaces profit, closure replaces opening, and the fall-off in patient base which is the foundation of a practice's goodwill, is fast at hand. The way to profit has never been greed or bad service, nor will it ever be."

Chapter 6:

Anatomy of Resistance

"Where there is power, there is resistance." Michel Foucault

Resilience trumps resistance every time. Getting from point A to point B, however, is a battle of wills, a clash of world-views, and any attachment to long-held values for the sake of being "right." The thirst for power and an addiction to control clouds good judgment and stalls out the possibilities inherent in needed change. In order to be resilient, one must first change his or her mind, and to do that you must first relinquish attachment to all of the above. Not easy. And resistance has a core engine that drives it forward: Fear.

So, what is there to be afraid of anyway?

Rosabeth Moss Kanter, a professor at Harvard Business School, illuminates, in The Harvard Business Review, the top reasons a good idea and the need for change can create powerful resistance and fear in even the best of us:

Resistance to change manifests itself in many ways, from foot-dragging and inertia, to petty sabotage, to outright rebellions. The best tool for leaders of change is to understand the predictable, universal sources of resistance.

Here are some of the top reasons that change and resistance go together, according to Kanter:

- **Loss of control**. Change interferes with our personal sense of autonomy and can make people feel that they've lost control over "their territory."

- **Excess uncertainty**. If change feels like walking off a cliff blindfolded, then people will reject it. People will often prefer to remain mired in misery than to head toward an unknown.

- **Everything seems different**. Change is meant to bring something different, but how different? We are creatures of habit. Routines become automatic, but change jolts us into consciousness, sometimes in uncomfortable ways.

- **Loss of face**. Change is a departure from the past and those people associated with the last version—the one that didn't work or is no longer working, or the one that's being superseded—are likely to be defensive about it. When change involves a big shift of strategic direction, the people responsible for the previous direction dread the perception that they may have been wrong.

- **More work**. Change is indeed more work. Those closest to the change in terms of designing and testing it are often overloaded, in part because of the inevitable unanticipated glitches in the middle of change and "everything can look like a failure in the middle," says Kanter.

- **Ripple effects**. Like tossing a pebble into a pond, change creates ripples.

Let me state the obvious about who feels the effects of change in dentistry most: The older, primarily Caucasian, males who have controlled the current medical and dental model for centuries. In fact, the patriarchal paradigm has been humming along for thousands of years and will not go quietly, even in the field of dentistry. This is simply the truth, not an indictment or a judgment.

The control and power that comes from being at the epicenter of any model for so long is now being challenged, and the solo practitioner is being questioned as to whether lack of efficiencies with the solo practitioner model are relevant or even wise in our changing times.

Older men have, in the past, controlled most of the powerful institutions, corporations, and media as they have done in medical and dental leadership. This is changing, however, with the emergence of a strong voice coming from women who not only are graduating from dental schools all across the nation, but also women who are CEOs, Deans, and leaders in the dental community.

So, we are not looking simply at a changing paradigm for dentistry; we are looking at a changing paradigm on a global scale across all industries and businesses. There is a competitive edge growing, which is one that the older autocratic dental model proponents put forth with force and it is their perceived fear of competition that sits at the center of the solo-DSO practice debate.

"People don't resist change. They resist being changed." Peter M. Senge

Chapter 7:

Relationships as Currency

Purpose or Profit: How About Both?

I mentioned earlier that one of the core distinctions at the heart of the DSO model is the emphasis on relationships: Relationships to the self, to the patient, and to the community, which are ethical and which create accountability as well as personal and group responsibility. So how can this emphasis on relationships lead to both profit and personal success as a practitioner?

In his book *Conscious Capitalism*, Whole Foods CEO John Mackey determines that relationships are the new model for good business in the 21st century. "*Conscious Capitalism* is a fairly new idea, but it's going to have a huge impact," Mackey begins by describing the philosophy he developed as he built his lone natural-foods store into an $8 billion retail mega beast. "I do believe it will become the dominant paradigm of all business in the 21st century." And he is right.

Conscious capitalism, Mackey insists, can move a corporation and even entire industries to refocus on *purpose.* In theory, conscious capitalism puts relationships at the helm of both good business and great profitability. This barn burning new model underscores the importance of attending to all of a company's (or practice's) interdependent stakeholders (employees, customers, suppliers, community, and the environment) in order to conduct good business.

In the conscious-capitalism model, profit is seen as a necessary outcome of doing business with heart, with people in mind, with service being central, and with quality and ethics mandatory. The developing DSO model supports all of this thinking. This proven holistic model has great relevance to the changing models in dentistry.

Our dental forefathers who had local family-run dental practices knew the power of personal and professional relationships with everyone in town. Sometimes they were the only dentists for more than one generation in a family, and back then your dentist was a trusted family ally. As we started the 21st century, however, this tightly knit form of dental practice gave way to less personal alliances and focused more and more on the financial thriving of the business, sometimes at the cost of relationships and the cost of the health and quality of life for the practitioner because insurance and technology demanded more and more time from practicing dentistry.

Another example of an industry, which is beginning to embrace conscious capitalism, is the banking world, which has some branches already moving in this direction. The International Finance Corporation (IFC), which is part of the World Bank Group, calls its new model "inclusive" and relational as well. Since 2005, IFC has committed over $11 billion dollars and worked with over 400 inclusive businesses in 90 countries to integrate more than 90 million people, including farmers, students, patients, utility customers, and micro borrowers, into core business operations. These investments are helping to improve lives, promote prosperity, and transform sustainable development outcomes in communities around the globe.

When all of those constituencies' interests are factored into the company's decisions and aligned, the way conscious capitalism thinking goes, is that "all, including - not incidentally - the bottom line, will flourish." The new bottom line becomes: Change your business model, and you effect change not only for your business and your bank account, but also for you personally, for your employees, and for your invested clients. The currency of relationships is becoming the best and wisest investment you can make. So, change an entire paradigm, which in turn transforms an industry, and you change the world just like Henry Ford did.

We can see examples like Henry Ford's innovative thinking already established in the dental community: Models for relational and inclusive dental practices that are supported by a DSO and there are numerous innovators and pioneers who have embraced the DSO - supported dental practice and have created innovative practices across the United States.

After graduating from UCLA in 1989, the current President of Pacific Dental Services (PDS), Stephen Thorne, found himself facing a difficult job market, so he started working with his dentist father in Victorville, California. "My father asked me to put a computer system in his office, and since I was pretty good with a computer, he asked me to digitize his dental practice," says Thorne in his article published in *DentalTown* in April 2014 entitled, "End of the Solo Era?"

Thorne continued working for his father and learning dental administration while helping grow the business from one to five practices. In 1993 Thorne took new ideas and an exciting vision and launched out on his own to create what he feels is the greatest dental company in America.

PDS was founded on a set of core values that distinguish the strength and character of the organization and direct all critical decisions. PDS believes:
- That lasting relationships are a key
- Constant learning and adaptability are part of their job
- Employees get paid based on their personal value to the
- company
- The way they conduct business is critical to whether business
- is good or bad
- The highest commitment to moral and ethical behavior,
- including honesty, integrity, and personal character, is central
- to doing good business
- Quality performance on every job, every day and every hour is
- required
- Everyone has the will to succeed and can make proper
- decisions
- They have an obligation and opportunity to present the best

- dentistry possible to each and every patient
- There is power in teamwork
-

Jeffrey Parker, CEO of DentaQuest Healthcare Delivery, recently became the first person associated with dentistry to make the annual HealthLeaders20 list and has long been cited for his work with Sarrell Dental in bringing dental care to 300,000 underserved children annually at its 15 clinics across Alabama. Sarrell remains the largest single provider of Medicaid dental services in Alabama. In an interview with DrBicuspid.com, Parker talks about this groundbreaking provider:

Ever since the PBS *Frontline* documentary '*Dollars and Dentists*' aired in June 2012, Sarrell has been in the national spotlight regarding our model of care. The *Frontline* piece was soon followed by positive reports on our model from the Robert Wood Johnson Foundation and by Forbes.com

As a result Sarrell Dental has gained enormous national attention in the past few years. Parker continues:

The attention to our model brought suitors from the for-profit side, private practice dentists, and dental chains. However, it also brought us a non-profit company that shares our goal of improving the oral health of everyone. Our two non-profits have joined together to help the underserved children and adults of our country.

Parker speaks also to what he thinks is keeping his model from expanding even further:

Regressive state dental practice acts. What I mean here is that it is absurd that a non-profit dental practice cannot be run by a non-dentist if they employ licensed dentists to perform the clinical work. However, more than 40 states currently restrict a non-profit dental practice, run by a businessperson, from cleaning teeth or filling cavities. I think any American would find a huge disconnect in the logic of most states' dental practice acts.

r innovative model is found in Affordable Dentures. The first Affordable Dentures dental practice opened in 1975 in Kinston, North Carolina, when founding dentists Dr. George Edwards, Jr. and Dr. Donald Henson saw a growing need in their community for dentures and tooth extractions at affordable fees.

The founders discovered the importance of providing immediate dentures with same-day service, especially for patients who traveled great distances, or for those who were taking time off work to receive treatment. Their same-day service approach made the practices unique. Today every affiliated practice has its own on-site denture lab to offer efficient, convenient dental care for patients.

Now with almost 200 affiliated practices in 40 states, the practice owner's benefit from the clinical and technical experiences they are able to share as a network of dental caregivers. Six million patients have received services from the affiliated practices providing Affordable Dentures.

The DSO model is not simply a solid, ethical, and lucrative inclusive business model for dentists, but it rides upon the rising tide of knowing that putting people and relationships at the center of your model is a win-win scenario and good business all the way around, as we have seen in these unique dental practice approaches.

And a DSO affords the dentist a chance to create and meet one of the most essential and universal needs for humans on the planet: Meaning.

So, I can hear you say, "What does meaning have to do with dentistry?"

Chapter 8:

The Meaningful Dentist

New emerging dentists are leading the way with a different set of values that has at the top of the list, quality of life, meaningful work, making a difference, family priorities, free time, and creative opportunity. The drive for money and power seems to be much further down the list of personal priorities and maybe this new emerging group of dentists understands that when you prioritize happiness, quality of life, and quality patient care, then the money will follow. These are meaningful values and suggest that there are more interior motives for being a dentist than that of simply having a well-paying job and secure retirement. The group that is in the lead for creating these values in their practices is the large number of women currently graduating from dental schools all over the nation and who have these values at the center of creating a thriving practice, many supported by a DSO.

The Search for Meaning

According to Kegan, *meaning making* is a lifelong activity that begins in infancy and continues to evolve through a series of stages encompassing childhood, adolescence, and adulthood for women and men alike. It is a core driver for everything we do in life, whether we are aware of it or not. It is behind the scenes of every decision we make, even if silently. When we stop searching for meaning, we have most likely succumb to falling prey to living with the prevailing meaning of our times and adopting it as our own, or allowing our culture to define our success, or that we have listened to our families, allowing them to create our world of meaning for us. Sound familiar?

And meaning does not have to be altruistic, humanitarian, emotional, psychological, or spiritual. Money, position, power, control, consumerism, hard work, providing for family, security, and prestige can also be just as meaningful for an individual. And the DSO model does not believe these values are mutually exclusive.

Discovering our own meaning in life and in work is key to knowing what makes us feel valued, what is of value to us, and what inspires and motivates us comes to a halt when we subscribe to what cultural norms call "success, prosperity, and even love." Certainly money, prestige, power, influence, or control can be meaningful to a person, but what the new generation is finding is that they are motivated more by relationships, quality of life, transformation, and intimate connection. They want more freedom. Emotional and spiritual values are finding their way into the work place and are driving goals for businesses and prosperity everywhere.

In the 1940's Abraham Maslow created a new awareness about what motivates all human behavior. He changed the face of sociology in doing so. His contribution, called *Maslow's Hierarchy of Needs* is taught around the world and remains one of the great systems to help understand the universal principles which motivate all that we do as humans, even at the workplace. Once the basic level of need is satisfied, we are universally driven to achieve the next level in our personal evolution. As an entire generation evolves to higher stages of motivation in life, paradigms for work and business must change, and we are seeing that right now in dentistry. As you might extrapolate from the following diagram, many businesses, as well as many institutions, are sorely stuck on one phase of meaning making: Safety. Playing it safe is a symptom of fear to move forward and in particular, fear of the unknown.

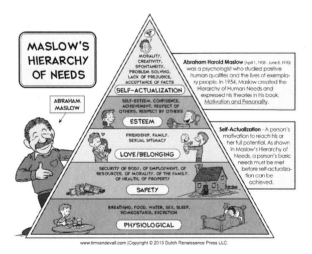

As humans, we need to make meaning of our existence. Meaning gives definition to our life and our life path. This search for meaning is often challenging but is also at the helm of all great paradigm shifts. How do we make sense of who we are within a world that seems out of balance with poverty, war, and famine on the one hand and tremendous privilege on the other? How do we as dentists, day in and day out, one crown or extraction after the other, retain the realization and the experience that we are changing lives? How can our vocation as dentists become transformative for everyone concerned when profit is no longer the bottom line, but rather the inevitable outgrowth of ethical, responsible relationships? When the business side of a dental practice is effectively and creatively managed, then the dentist has time to address these essential questions that in the end makes them a far better practitioner.

One innovative model is found in the Dentists Without Borders program, which has found a way to make meaning in the world with dental expertise. Almost 100% of the rural population and a vast majority of the poor population living in urban areas of underdeveloped nations have absolutely no dental care. This translates into billions of people. A volunteer dentist who has been in the frontlines for almost 30 years has noted, "I have seen lines of people three blocks long waiting to receive dental care. These people are emergency cases and are in pain. Many who are unable to get in the doors of the clinic that day will stay in line all night to get in the next day."

Closer to home, there are the Missions of Mercy programs. There is no more poignant example of meaning and crafting a work ethic to change lives, than the Crying Corner.

Picture 800 volunteers, 400 dentists, 400 helpers, and a crowd of people who stand in line all day to receive free dental help from the volunteer dentist. The line goes out the door and down the block. There are some with nearly no teeth or rotting teeth who are ultimately fitted for dentures. The moment these people see their own faces smiling back at them for the very first time, some sob with shock, surprise, gratitude, and relief. I have seen both patient and provider crying and hugging-that's meaningful.

This example of creating meaning as a dentist is part of the fabric of traditional solo practice and the new DSO model. With a DSO handling the business side of a practice, however, the dentist has more free time to give back to society in new ways and has time to volunteer and make an even greater difference with their skills.

So, the byproduct of the DSO model is that for the dentist who has been piled high with paperwork, marketing, and running a business can now become the dentist who can focus on creating great patient care and ongoing relationships. In the end, patients feel taken care of, the dentist is given a gift of having more time to give back to society, his or her happiness excels while self-esteem increases. This is simply good for all concerned.

"Nothing truly valuable can be achieved except by the unselfish cooperation of many individuals." — Albert Einstein

Religions and philosophies have pondered the question of meaning as a core tenet for their framework of beliefs. There are as many answers, from materialism, to community, to spirituality, as there are humans to think of them. Physicians and dentists are no less immune to this question as monks or priests. For each one of these institutions, these roles are there to serve the greater whole. The community members and the profits that come from strong doctor-patient connections are increased exponentially when we make our relationships key. This approach is a model that women in business understand and, more often than not, support, and it is emerging all over the world: The model of inclusion.

"Patriarchy is like the elephant in the room that we don't talk about, but how could it not affect the planet radically when it's the superstructure of human society." – A. DiFranco

In 2013, as reported in Harvard Business Review, John Gerzema wrote an article entitled, *Female Values Can Give Tomorrow's Leaders an Edge"*, which states:

A Pew Center study released in May of 2013 revealed that working mothers are the sole or primary providers in a record 40% of U.S. households. Only a few days before, hedge fund billionaire Paul Tudor-Jones created a stir by remarking at a conference that women will never rival men (as traders) because babies are a "focus killer."

Here we have the dynamics of a new economy colliding with the old establishment like tectonic plates. But as developed nations restructure from manufacturing to knowledge and services, my bet is on the moms, or more specifically, on women — and men who can think like them. My colleague Michael D'Antonio and I gathered from 64,000 people in nationally representative samples in 13 countries—from the Americas and Europe to Asia—point to widespread dissatisfaction with typically "male" ways of doing business and a growing appreciation for the traits, skills and competencies that are perceived as more female.

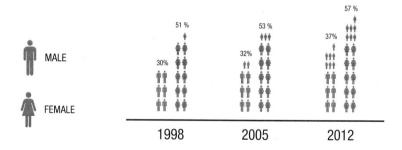

PERCENT OF DENTISTS UNDER 35 WHO ARE EMPLOYEES

American Dental Association, Health Policy Institute, 2014

Let's not fail to address that women are graduating from dental schools in unprecedented numbers and will impact the industry, as well as many women will adopt the DSO model since it is in keeping with some of their personal commitments and values. The values that many female dentists bring to the table we will refer to as *inclusive*. Inclusive suggest a group focus centered on the community and on consensus verses power and control, which is more exclusive.

Although this model feels new, it is rooted in some of the most powerful tribal collective wisdom that we are simply remembering and not inventing anew inside of dentistry.

"A tribe is a group of people connected to one another, connected to a leader, and connected to an idea. For millions of years, human beings have been part of one tribe or another. A group needs only two things to be a tribe: a shared interest and a way to communicate." Seth Godin, *Tribes: We Need You to Lead Us*

The current notion of patriarchal rule is under siege. The solo practice model is entrenched in this many thousands-year-old paradigm and has been disintegrating now for decades, without its consent. Money, power, and control no longer are sustainable as central drivers for any business model. We see this in most developing countries, which are rising up with a new voice for equality and change. Politics that focus on control and power-over and which leads to greed and corruption are no longer sustainable. The healthcare and dental community are not immune to these factors.

As we face nearly 50% of all graduates from dental schools being women who possibly understand and value a model of inclusion, the new model is right on time and requires our attention.

Chapter 9:

The New Leadership

Let's take a look at the emerging new business model for effective leadership, which goes hand in hand with the changing, more inclusive, paradigm for dentistry. Any transitioning model needs new leaders who are adept at moving between the old model and the new to bridge the resisters and the game changers and do it with a set of new skills. This is always challenging. This leadership skill set has a new core component: *Emotional intelligence*. Emotional intelligence began as psychological theory and was developed by Peter Salovey and John Mayer, who in 1997 wrote,

Emotional intelligence is the ability to perceive emotions, to access and generate emotions so as to assist thought, to understand emotions and emotional knowledge, and to reflectively regulate emotions so as to promote emotional and intellectual growth.

Peter Salovey is the President of Yale University. With John D. Mayer, he developed a broad framework called emotional intelligence. The theory says that as people have a wide range of intellectual abilities, they also have a wide range of measurable emotional skills that profoundly affect their thinking and actions. The core tenants of Salovey and Mayer regarding emotional intelligence, which subsequently fueled an innovative new business and leadership model, can be seen below in the comparison they created.

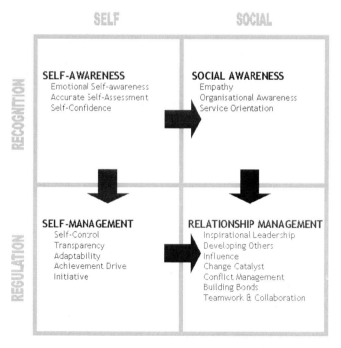

Published in Emotional Intelligence by Daniel Goleman, 2005

Daniel Goleman first brought the term emotional intelligence to a wider audience with his 1995 book of the same name. Goleman, a science journalist, who brought *Emotional Intelligence* to the bestseller list, has authored a number of books on the subject, including *Working With Emotional Intelligence*, and, recently *Social Intelligence: The New Science of Human Relationships*. This body of work relates to the growing edge we are straddling in dentistry.

Goleman applied this concept to business practices in his 1998 Harvard Business Review article. In his research studying nearly 200 large, global companies, Goleman found that while the qualities traditionally associated with leadership, such as intelligence, toughness, determination, and vision, are required for success, they are not sufficient. He discovered that truly effective leaders are also distinguished by a high degree of emotional intelligence, which includes self-awareness, self-regulation, motivation, empathy, and social skills. For this new model to firmly take hold, we need leaders well versed in this leadership skill set.

These qualities may sound soft and un-business-like, but Goleman found direct ties between emotional intelligence and measurable positive business outcomes. While emotional intelligence's relevance to business has continued to ignite debate over years, Goleman's article remains the definitive reference on the subject, including his description of each component of emotional intelligence and a detailed discussion of how to recognize it in potential leaders, how and why it connects to performance, and how it can be learned. Goleman notes:

The most effective leaders are alike in one crucial way: They all have a high degree of what has come to be known as emotional intelligence. It's not that IQ and technical skills are irrelevant. They do matter, but mainly as threshold capabilities; that is, they are the entry-level requirements for executive positions. But my research, along with other recent studies, clearly shows that emotional intelligence is the sine qua non of leadership. Without it, a person can have the best training in the world, an incisive, analytical mind, and an endless supply of smart ideas, but he still won't make a great leader.

As we construct a new emerging model for dentistry with the new and powerful building blocks of conscious capitalism, ethics, purpose, meaning, relationships, inclusion, and accountability, as well as emotional intelligence - all of which lead to larger profits and greater client satisfaction then the leadership for this model will need to be cut from a different cloth.

Here are the five components Goleman say that an emotionally intelligent leader needs to employ, according to Goleman, as was published in the Harvard Business Review.

The Five Components of Emotional Intelligence at Work

	Definition	Hallmarks
Self-Awareness	the ability to recognize and understand your moods, emotions, and drives, as well as their effect on others	self-confidence realistic self-assessment self-deprecating sense of humor
Self-Regulation	the ability to control or redirect disruptive impulses and moods the propensity to suspend judgment – to think before acting	trustworthiness and integrity comfort with ambiguity openness to change
Motivation	a passion to work for reasons that go beyond money or status a propensity to pursue goals with energy and persistence	strong drive to achieve optimism, even in the face of failure organizational commitment
Empathy	the ability to understand the emotional makeup of other people skill in treating people according to their emotional reactions	expertise in building and retaining talent cross-cultural sensitivity service to clients and customers
Social Skill	proficiency in managing relationships and building networks an ability to find common ground and build rapport	effectiveness in leading change persuasiveness expertise in building and leading teams

• **Self-awareness** is the ability to recognize and understand personal moods, emotions, and drives, as well as their effect on others. Examples of self-awareness include self-confidence, realistic self-assessment, and a self-deprecating sense of humor. Self-awareness depends on one's ability to monitor one's own emotional state.

• **Self Regulation** is the ability to control or redirect disruptive impulses and moods and is the propensity to suspend judgment and to think before acting. Hallmarks include trustworthiness and integrity; comfort with ambiguity; and openness to change.

- **Internal Motivation** is a passion to work for internal reasons that go beyond money and status such as an inner vision of what is important in life, a joy in doing something, a curiosity in learning, and a propensity to pursue goals with energy and persistence. Hallmarks include a strong drive to achieve, optimism even in the face of failure, and organizational commitment.

- **Empathy** is the ability to understand the emotional makeup of other people - a skill in treating people according to their emotional reactions. Examples include expertise in building and retaining talent, cross-cultural sensitivity, and service to clients and customers.

- **Social Skills** include a proficiency in managing relationships and building networks, and an ability to find common ground and build rapport. Hallmarks of social skills include effectiveness in leading change, persuasiveness, and expertise building and leading teams.

The changing trends in dentistry, which not only include a new model for dentistry and dental practices, but also require new leadership to stand behind this new model, are only one additional challenge facing dentists and their practices.

We have mentioned the new breed of dentist emerging from a growing number of dental schools and an unprecedented gender shift within dentistry, which may single-handedly make change mandatory in the dental community. Let's look at each of the game-changing variables and how they impact the dentist and his or her practice, including the changing consumer.

Chapter 10:

A New Breed of Dentist

As previously mentioned, today nearly half the new dentists graduating from schools all over the country are female. Students leave school more in debt than ever before. Buying a practice is no longer as viable or preferable. The patients are taking charge of their own care and dentists need to respond. The DSO model understands that there is a new landscape that every new dentist steps into upon graduation, which begs new questions and innovative answers and that the solo practice model is not the direction the new dentist is taking.

Debt and New Values

Growing school debt and different lifestyle choices for new dentists are influencing practice choices fresh out of school. As of 2013, here are the top trends for the new dentist, according to the American Dental Association article *Critical Trends Affecting the Future of Dentistry*:

• The school debt load of new dental graduates has grown to an average of approximately $200,000 and more

• More than four out of ten dental school seniors say that educational debt has a great influence on their professional choices after graduation

• The new dentist is more likely to forgo solo practices for joint, group, or corporate practices

• Dentists who have completed their dental education within the past ten years are three times more likely to be part of a larger company than those who completed their education more than ten years ago

• A growing number of couples are entering dentistry with even larger debt burdens, making the purchase of a practice even more difficult. On the other hand, the couples can both work part-time and still have sufficient family income with a DSO supported practice

• New dentists are choosing to work fewer hours and
      pursue other personal activities (i.e., quality of life trumps
      overworking)

These new dentists are bringing with them a desire for balance in their lives. Many dentists do not want to work as much, wanting instead to have quality family time and leisure time, as well as wanting to do what is needed to create a life they want to live outside of the office. Their drive for success is tempered by a set of values that insists on a quality of life with meaning and an emphasis on the family. Long overworked hours are no longer acceptable since the new generation has different values and goals than those from the past. The younger generation doesn't want to work as much since dentistry is stressful and requires minute attention. So "work enough to do what you want" is the new perspective.

The Female Dentist

The article "*Critical Trends Affecting the Future of Dentistry*" goes on to report that there is a wave of female dentists surging through dentistry that is responsible for some of the largest shifts in dentistry history. Nearly 40% percent of new, professionally active dentists (graduated dental school within past 10 years) are female, compared to 22 % percent of all professionally active dentists. Sixty percent of dentists under the age of 44 are women. Women are more likely to practice part-time (less than 30 hours a week). New female active private practitioners are also less likely to be owner dentists and more likely to be associates or employees.

There is no turning back this tide. The impact that this gender-shift will have on dentistry is only just now being understood. A logical starting place is to look at the demographics of women in dentistry over the past few decades in order to understand the impact that women will now have in a dental practice and why the DSO model is suited to this growing edge of female dentists.

In the 2008 publication *Inside Dentistry*, Dominic Saadi, MA, researched some interesting statistics regarding the shifting of gender in dentistry." Saadi reports that prior to the early 1970s dentists were almost exclusively male. America had the lowest percentage of female dentists in the western world. Around the same time, roughly half of the dentists in Greece were women, about one-third in France, Denmark, Sweden, and Norway, and almost four-fifths in Russia, Finland, Latvia, and Lithuania. Two reasons led to this gender shift in our country: The first reason was women's liberation and the civil rights movements of the 1960s and early 1970s, which resulted in federally legislated funding of grants that encouraged increasing enrollments of women in professional health schools. The second reason was the impact that the introduction of birth control had on opening the doors for a woman into a professional career since most women could then choose when to have children.

We need to ask how women will impact the psycho-graphic, social, cultural, developmental, psychological, and attitudinal aspects in dentistry. What questions are now on the table to be explored, and what new procedures, models, and expectations will need to be created to support this powerfully growing group of female dentists?

Lynn Carlisle, DDS has written a book and developed a web site on a new model of healthcare based on developing exceptional, caring doctor-patient relationships. His book, *In the Spirit of Caring*, gives dentists information and ideas on how to implement this new model and reclaim or improve this vital relationship with patients. Dr. Carlisle also worked on a survey in conjunction with the ADA, from which he suggests that the following questions are at the heart of this demographic gender shift and when addressed, will change the face of dentistry in a way that has never been considered before. He asks the following questions that we are all thinking:

1. The vast majority of research, opinions, and surveys on what makes an outstanding dentist have been done by white males about other white males. Does this research apply to women? What applies and what does not? Will the female inclusive model replace the masculine exclusive model in dentistry?

2. Are women naturally better at creating relationships, especially doctor– client relationships, or do they have the same challenges that men do in creating these relationships?

3. Does dental school education stifle the spirit of caring in women as it has in men?

4. What are the unique challenges that women dentists face?

5. Are women naturally better at relationship-based dentistry than men?

6. Is the personality profile of women dentists the same as for men?

7. Will the demands of motherhood derail or change the woman dentist's dental career plans?

8. What impact will women have when they are the majority or near majority of dentists?

9. Will fewer women dentists elect to have their own practice and choose to work for someone else?

10. Will different practice models be created to accommodate the different needs of women who are dentists? What will they look like?

11. Will many women dentists refuse to seek higher levels of training in restorative and relationship-based dentistry because this type of commitment unbalances their life too much?

12. Will creative solutions be developed to address the unique demands of being a woman dentist?

These questions posed by Dr. Carlisle are not only politically provocative, but they bring to the forefront of the shifting dental model the core questions, to which the answers will shape both private practices and group practice in the future.

The DSO and large group practices are great for women for the following reasons:

• Women are typically more community and relationship based at large, which is inherent in the DSO model.
• Community and group practices let women step right in and find the values that are meaningful for them while offering needed support.
• A group practice that is DSO-supported offers the collaboration and competition that keeps a dentist on a cutting edge while affording them the time to achieve a higher quality of life.

There are numerous female dentists who started as solo practitioners, and in the early years of the DSO model found that this was the support they had been wanting. A perfect example of this is Dr. Nelly Barreto, who after years in her New Jersey private dental practice felt she needed a big change. In my interview with Dr. Barreto, she said,

I had my own practice in New Jersey for 14 years. But, the weights of running the business and being a good dentist were in conflict. I simply needed more time at home with my family. I needed to enjoy dentistry more than I was. And, as you know, when you are a solo practitioner you are married to your practice. I would get home to my husband and two small children and have to face an evening of paperwork. My love of my work with my patients was diluted because I had so much of the business to run. My quality of life with my family was taking a back seat to maintaining my solo practice. I had wanted to be a dentist since I was seven, but it was so much work, and I was missing out on my children's childhoods.

Then I saw an advertisement in an ADA journal, which caught my eye. This was the only advertisement in the journal for a DSO. It was called Perfect Teeth and at that moment I realized that this DSO might be the answer for me. With Perfect Teeth I got to love dentistry again.

So, I sold my practice and moved to Colorado Springs, Colorado, and began working with Perfect Teeth, which gave me leeway to manage my practice. That was nearly 15 years ago. It was a fabulous choice. They do the training and all the administrative aspects so I can focus on dentistry. Another plus with this DSO is that I have community. I have had support from other dentists who stepped in and helped me when my dad passed away. I just asked for help and there they were. That would not have been able to happen in my solo practice.

I feel that any criticism of the DSO model is simply because of lack of information. I am involved in dentistry on a local and state level and I do believe with education and good clear answers the perceptions are now changing and the DSO model is being seen as the great support for dentists that it is. It is all about perceptions, which need to change. In many ways I believe that the DSO model is saying, "we are here and we are here to stay."

For me, the business support has given me greater stability as a dentist, allowed me focus on dentistry, and provided exceptional patient care. They handle the administrative side of the business, which for the first 14 years of my private practice kept me from the things I truly valued. This was a perfect choice for me and I feel it is a great option for young dentists who want the support of older dentists as their mentors and teachers. Since quality of life is so important to me, and enjoying what I do as a dentist is equally important, I see no disadvantages to the DSO model. I am a better dentist and a better manager with employees that feel like family.

Chapter 11:

Why Change?

In the first part of this book, we looked at the variables that are demanding that the dental model change for the betterment of dentistry. We have seen that there are complex factors that are pushing for us to create unity and understanding as this new model is birthed. Space needs to be made for the new idea, the new model, and the new direction to take a foothold. So, the death throws of an entire approach to solo practice in dentistry are heard loud and clear. Without death there is no new life. Enter the power struggle between the old paradigm and the new for us as dentists.

We have looked at the inherent fears and resistances in the changing world of dentistry and have had a glimpse of why the dental landscape is changing and requiring a new response. There are some critical trends worth looking at as we work toward creating unity in the dental community.

The Changing Dental Environment

In 2013, D.A. Diringer and Associates published paper entitled *Critical Trends Affecting the Future of Dentistry*, exposing some valuable statistics regarding changes in dentistry. Diringer and Associates feel that the landscape of dentistry in the United States is in a moment of radical transformation. The general population is aging and becoming more diverse, which has contributed to rapid changes as well. Consumer habits are shifting and patients are relying on technology more and more while seeking greater value for their spending. Along with this, the nature of oral disease and the financing of dental care are in a state of massive change. So what does the research reveal?

A Busy Practice

A staggering one third of all dentists are no longer busy enough, which is a direct hit to potential earnings and growing a practice. Part of this may be due to the lack of ease with assertive marketing in order to create new clientele while trying to wear all hats that are required to run a solo practice. Group practices have far more marketing power and marketing dollars at their disposal, but the solo practitioner burns the candle at both ends, trying to offer great patient care and run a complex business single handedly.

Debt and the Private Practice

There is also a changing pattern within dentistry itself, in that there is a notable expansion of new dental schools. With this expansion comes a new dilemma: Debt. As we have discussed, debt from school limits the options for a new dentist to purchase a retiring dentist's practice, and, as I have mentioned, banks are not taking risks on large school debts coupled with the price of buying an existing practice. As a result, this issue then creates a new concern: Dentists who have counted on the sale of their practices in order to retire are simply not able to retire when and how they had expected. The assurance of the retirement fund that many dentists depend on to retire is no longer an assurance. Today, the average age for a dentist to retire is 69-years old.

The Overall Impact on the Dental Profession

Writing for the *Journal of the California Dental Association*, Dr. Richard T. Kao states,

Effective practice management has become progressively more difficult for solo practice owners. Healthcare professionals work in a stress-filled environment, and dentists are not immune. Increased government regulations, rising supply costs, and competitive labor markets have made practice overhead difficult to contain.

Rising technology costs and reductions in employer-sponsored dental insurance coverage are creating dissatisfaction among dentists in regards to the business-side of their profession. Kao adds:

For many years, dentists have complained that the biggest challenges to being a dentist have nothing to do with clinical aspects, and while dental students have been taught to diagnose and treat dental disease, little time is spent preparing these students to own and operate a small business, even though the majority of dentists eventually do own and manage their own practices.

In November 2013, the *Dental Economics/Levin Group 7th Annual Practice Research Report* noted, "one-third of survey respondents indicated that their greatest challenge is finding ways to increase practice production and profit. Another third of dentists report that inefficient practice systems are the primary barriers to success." The survey also reported that more than a third of general practice dentists utilize the assistance of consultants or coaches for assistance in practice restructuring and development. The central demand in the profession seems singular: *practice management relief.*

The results of the ADA's *2012 Group Practice Survey* reveal that "work-life balance, flexible schedule, guaranteed salary, and less interaction with insurance companies, appear to be perceived benefits of *relief* from some of the time and effort spent on managing a traditional solo practice or partnership."

The article, *Toward a Common Goal: The Role of Dental Support Organizations in an Evolving Profession*, goes on to discuss why DSOs offer an important additional choice for dentists faced with the practice management challenges described above and why individual dentists should be free to decide the path they will follow:

Many will continue to opt for the independence afforded by a traditional solo practice, while others are likely to consider DSO models as the avenue for meeting their personal and professional needs.

In a free market economy, dentists who choose to focus more time on patient care than practice management should have the ability to consider the arrangement best suited to their objectives.

We have found that in the last ten years significant increases in the number of female dentists entering the profession coupled with the heightened debt of all dental graduates have produced a dramatic shift in the career paths of dentists. The availability of DSO affiliation represents a critical option to enable new and veteran dentists to reduce the time and expense associated with practice operations and focus more time on patient care.

Dentists who can benefit from practicing in a DSO environment include:

- *Part-timers* – Dentists who prefer to practice only on a part time basis can easily find employment in a practice supported by a DSO. This often is an attractive alternative for female dentists who desire to start a family or a dentist who is closer to retirement and who does not desire to practice 40 hours a week.

- *Recent Dental School Graduates* –DSO affiliation represents a viable option for the new dentist to open their own practices earlier in their careers, rather than practicing as a veteran dentist's associate.

Today, dentists increasingly begin their practice careers with significant debt from student loans. Some dental school graduates are simply unwilling or unable to take out a loan to finance a new practice on top of already significant student loan obligations. As the U.S. economy continues its slow rebound, DSO financing provides a viable option at a time when industries are looking for investors and capital and states are looking for new avenues of job creation as well as increased access to dental services.

There are three primary funding options that exist for new dentists seeking to finance a new dental practice: (1) self-funding; (2) arranging financing through banks or other lenders; and (3) utilizing financing options through a DSO.

• ***Dentists with Limited Business Acumen*** – Dental schools provide comparatively little training with respect to the challenges of owning and operating a small business. Skilled dental practitioners who may have not been successful as small business owners can now own practices with the nonclinical support they need.

In general, trends among new dentists favoring the option of working with a DSO-supported dental practice parallel trends among young physicians who are more than 30 times more likely to choose hospital employment over a solo practice, according to a Merritt Hawkins Survey. Like young dentists, young physicians worry about the risk and expense entailed in starting their own practice in the face of massive student loan debt. Young physicians are increasingly gravitating toward the stability of hospital employment, and physicians looking to start families place considerable importance on work-life balance."

The DSO-supported practice can handle large volumes of patients and can demonstrate efficiency and improved outcomes. Metrics are increasingly important to public payers. As these *accountable care organizations* mature under health reform, they will begin to seek the inclusion of oral health and seek the same measures of outcomes, quality, and efficiency. The large practices are likely to grow as the demands for what is called *triple aim* increases:

• Improved experience of care
• Improved population health
• Reduced per capita costs

As we watch this tipping point in dentistry stir up a storm of responses, we cannot become complacent. Educating ourselves to create clear responses to new questions without reactivity and fear is a number one mandate in a shifting industry. When we can be clear on what key forces are at work, we can assist the profession in defining its own destiny. To ignore what is happening in health and consumer environments will be to abdicate the power for change to the next generation of dentists. And while this next generation is coming on the scene with new values and objectives, there is no greater shift in this dental landscape than within the consumers group.

Chapter 12:

The New Consumer

The consumer is now exercising power in his or her own healthcare like never before. Consumers are concerned with value, quality, and convenience. Consumers are asking new questions and demanding they be answered. They have social media at their fingertips and are arming themselves with awareness of their rights to quality and value in their dental and medical care.

The new consumer is focused on getting more value in his or her experience and having convenience to home and work life while using the internet to compare practitioner reviews in order to insure quality of work. The new consumer also possesses a desire for more personal face-to-face interactions coupled with innovation in care as one of his or her greatest drivers.

The Power of the Consumer

Consumers are becoming more astute purchasers of oral healthcare. Consumers are becoming clearer in their decision-making regarding their own healthcare, their spending, and their imperative for value in their choices. Even the word "patient" is being stigmatized and the American population wants to view themselves not as healthcare consumers, or even as discerning clients but as educated persons invested in their own healthcare. They voice new and different expectations, needs, and wants in their dental care.

So we might even go one step further when referring to patients or consumers. We may want to focus on the individuals that we care for, not as those who are consuming our services or who are ill, but as individuals who have taken a *vested interest* in their own future, their own healthcare, and their family's wellbeing as they speak up for what they need. The age of the doctor being the all-knowing-one is over, and we have entered a time within dentistry and medicine in which the individual and the doctor are collaborators. The power model has changed as well, from an exclusive model to an inclusive one, as we have discussed earlier.

So, for all intents and purposes, I will refer to the patient and the consumer now as the *invested client*. Each individual who seeks dental care has a growing vested interest in their own pocket book, in the quality of their care, in their rights, and their expectations for value of service.

The New Holy Grail for the Invested Client

For the invested client there are three primary questions regarding which dentist is right for them, what procedure is necessary, and how much they are willing to spend:

• Value

• Convenience

• Quality of care

As a result, these changing needs for value, convenience, and quality are demanding innovation and adaptation, especially with invested clients holding the new power of technology, allowing them to demand quality care and affordability that will impact every dentist at every level. Technology has changed how a client shops for his or her dental needs, they have new ways of instantly comparing quality and price and with this information, comes power.

The Older Invested Client

Older invested clients generally want personal interactions with providers. They are eager to speak with a real person, have a friend refer them, and get to know a secretary or a hygienist. However, baby boomers may soon become more concerned with cost as they join the ranks of the elderly, who will have less coverage and more out-of-pocket costs for their care, which makes it important to get greater value for their money.

The Role of Dental Support Organizations for the New Invested Client

Numerous publications have discussed the current state of affairs for the dental profession in the United States. Articles address the challenges ahead and the role of DSOs in mitigating the changes we are facing.

According to the ADA, more than 181 million Americans will not visit a dentist in 2014.

Like physicians who have aligned with management services organizations (MSOs), dentists supported by DSOs are able to focus on treating their patients and providing affordable care—particularly for populations such as working-age adults, the young, and the poor. MSOs and DSOs allow physicians and dentists to be more attentive to patient care and allow knowledgeable business professionals to assist with the nonclinical administration of the practice. By spending their time more efficiently, dentists who hire DSOs are able to deliver dental services at lower prices, thereby increasing the accessibility of dental care to wider communities in which they practice. These approaches directly speak to the new values and the new power held by the invested client.

Patient Care is the Responsibility of the Dentist

The thousands of dentists who choose to practice in a DSO model maintain the same requirements and professional standards as dentists who perform administrative and business tasks themselves or with the assistance of multiple service vendors and consultants. As the Academy of General Dentistry (AGD) notes:

Regardless of who holds the responsibility for business decisions, dentists hold the responsibility for their clinical and ethical decisions, whether before a state dental board, a court of law, or the court of public opinion…regardless of practice modality, the ultimate responsibility for compliance with state laws and regulations falls upon the licensed dentist.

When referencing DSOs, certain spokespersons confuse the discussion through the use of inflammatory phrases such as "corporate dentistry" or "private equity." These critics infer that a dental practice hiring a DSO violates its legal, moral, and ethical duties by transferring responsibility for all patient-care decisions to the DSO. To the contrary: at all times dental practices supported by a DSO, like many sole-practitioner arrangements, are owned entirely by licensed dentists who are expressly responsible for patient care.

Technology
The new consumer is also benefited by the growing edge of technology in dentistry.

Mandates in the Affordable Care Act, state laws, and the innovative nature of dentistry are moving the profession to commit to electronic health records, CAD / CAM technologies, digital diagnostics, and more—all of which benefit patients. Unless a dentist is independently wealthy or has the means to afford bank loans to fund these investments, the dentist and his or her invested clients may have to do without such technologies.

DSOs are able to invest in those needed and innovative technologies and invest in new practices with financial terms that dentists of even those with moderate means can now afford. These financial resources help promote greater efficiency and expand access to care for the benefit of patients and dentists alike and without requiring tax dollars to accomplish these objectives. Private equity represents a free-market solution within the dental profession—as it has with hospital companies, ambulatory surgery centers, and others—at a time when government reimbursement for dental care is significantly lower than for general healthcare services.

Clinical vs. Nonclinical

In a 2014 ADSO report entitled *The Role of Dental Support Organizations in an Evolving Profession*, the changes in dentistry and the question of clinical verses nonclinical responsibilities were addressed:

The dental profession is faced with significant challenges while the United States contends with a national oral healthcare crisis. Dental support organizations offer vital assistance in the fight against oral disease, providing dentists with a single source for practice administration and development resources, training, financing, and other nonclinical services that would otherwise involve numerous vendors or hours of the practitioners' valuable—and limited—time. Today's dentists must navigate mounting debt from student and practice loans as well as increasing liability and compliance requirements. DSOs provide a way for dentists to reduce the time, expense, and stress associated with the administrative aspects of their practices provide care for a wider community base, including patients who have been previously underserved. Through collaboration with the ADA, the AGD, and other leading professional organizations, the ADSO is committed to assisting dentists in a common goal—the improvement of oral health in the United States through the accessibility of high-quality dental care. Put another way, the DSO model enables dentists to focus their time on patients—not paperwork.

Every state's dental laws make it perfectly clear that in matters of patient care, a dentist licensed in that state and regulated by its dental board is responsible for the clinical side of the practice, which may include operational tasks that can be performed by any individual. How the dentist-owner of a practice chooses to handle administrative needs is left to the individual.

The Issue of Ownership

In *Toward a Common Goal: The Role of Dental Support Organizations in an Evolving Profession*, it is made clear that opposition to the DSO model seeks "to create the inference" that a dental practice that hires a DSO violates its legal, moral, and ethical duties by transferring responsibility for all clinical decisions in that dental practice to the DSO. The structure and legality of the DSO arrangement with respect to the corporate practice of dentistry prohibition is no different than many sole practitioner arrangements. A professional corporation or other professional entity owns the dental practice. Pursuant to state law, the shareholders of this professional corporation must be licensed dentists. This means that the dental professional entity then employs or contracts, as independent contractors, the dental service providers.

The shareholder dentists or dentist owners are at all times responsible for the care rendered by the dental practice. This professional entity then also contracts with a DSO for administrative services. At all times, dentists (not a lay corporate entity) are responsible for the dental care provided by the dental practice. The dental practice employs or contracts with all dentists. DSOs do not employ or contract dentists for dental services. As a result of these factors, the term "corporate dentistry" in no way describes a DSO.

Much the same as with the term 'corporate dentistry', these opponents further attempt to disparage dentists who hire DSOs by noting that many DSOs are owned by a private equity or perhaps other investors who then will "control" the DSO-supported dentist. A private equity typically consists of funds (similar to and including mutual funds and pension plans) in which many investors pool their monies to invest in companies that are not listed on a national stock exchange. The investors in private equity funds include people from all walks and stations in life, such as a teachers' union pension plan.

Most companies in the United States are not listed on public stock exchanges, although private equity funds may also invest in publically traded companies. In other words, many Americans are invested in funds that have investments in DSOs, which certain commentators attempt to demonize as private equities.

Both DSO-supported and traditional dental practices commonly utilize the services of non-dentists for a wide range of operational tasks, such as:

• Accounting and tax preparation

• Payroll administration and processing

• Payor relations

• Billing and collections

• Human resources

The fundamental difference between dental practices supported by DSOs and those not supported by DSOs is not the type of administrative services performed by the licensed dentist. The difference is that the DSO outsources administrative tasks and other nonclinical services through a single source, while the practices not supported by a DSO use either internal resources and or a number of outside vendors and consultants to perform such tasks and services.

Increasing Access to Care

In the report *Oral Health in America*, published in 2000, former Surgeon General David Satcher speaks on the "silent epidemic of oral diseases affecting our most vulnerable citizens: poor children, the elderly, and many members of racial and ethnic minority groups." DSO-supported dentists already play an important role in the national fight against oral disease. In a 2012 policy brief reported in the article *Dental Visits for Medicaid Children,* Burton L. Edelstein, DDS, MPH, estimated that DSO-supported dentists provided more than one-fifth of dental care services to children on Medicaid in 2009. Edelstein went on to say that the DSO business model is "able to reduce operating costs" and provide flexible scheduling that recognizes the "impediments that many low-income families face with transportation and work arrangements."

It is also stated in *Toward a Common Goal: The Role of Dental Support Organizations in an Evolving Profession*, that DSO-supported practices not only increase access to care, but also provide value to tax-payers. They contribute to:

• Lower overhead costs, which enable DSO-supported dentists to accept insurance from a broader range of payers, both public and private

• They have helped open states manage care plans

• DSO-supported practices charged, on average, 11% less than traditional practitioners

• DSO-supported dental practices are frequently located in underserved areas, providing lower-income populations with treatment options close to home

• Patients of DSO-supported practices have consistently given their experience high marks on patient satisfaction surveys

Impact on the Dentist

The impact for the dentist in a changing dental environment is also discussed at length in the article, *Toward a Common Goal*:

The challenges of governmental regulations, along with rising supply and technology costs and reductions in employer-sponsored dental insurance coverage, are producing dissatisfaction among dentists with the business side of their profession. These caregivers are increasingly tasked to manage student loan debt, malpractice liability, and practice compliance rather than prioritize the needs of their patients. The central demand in the profession seems singular: practice management relief.

DSOs offer an important choice for dentists faced with these practice management challenges. Many will continue to opt for the independence of a traditional solo practice, whereas others are likely to consider DSO models for meeting their personal and professional needs. In a free market economy, dentists who choose to focus more time on patient care than on the challenges posed by practice administration should have the ability to consider the arrangement best suited to their objectives.

Chapter 13:

The DSO-Supported Solo Practitioner

Often, dentists have several dental practices plugging away at the same time. My experience is that to accomplish this feat, they have had to compromise heavily to manage the tidal wave of detail to keep each boat afloat. They may have more earnings by managing these multiple practices, but at what cost?

Placing their practice support into one central entity could make sense. An example of centralizing the business support could be using one office manager for all the practices instead of one for each practice and creating an in-house accounting and billing department instead of paying an outside firm who charges a monthly fee. Once this process is initiated, they may find that the golden ticket lies in the creation of standardized efficiencies with one integrated practice system for all the offices. Forming a DSO as part of an exit-strategy could be an economically feasible option, just as it is a smart move to abandon the solo practice model when arriving at several dental practices in your portfolio.

Individual Versus Group Practices

By their very nature, solo practices force the dentist to wear all the business hats. With the solo practice model, as you will see in the following graphic, the core work for the solo practice dentist is at the center of the graphic and includes a staggering number of responsibilities outside the scope of patient care. The burden of trying to carry all of these administrative responsibilities is the skill set of a DSO.

SOLO PRACTIONER TIME ALLOCATION

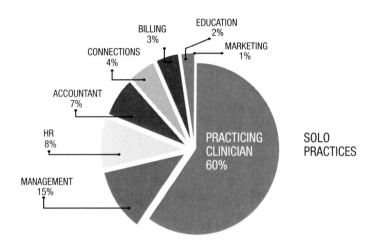

In comparison, let's look at how the support of a DSO changes everything.

DSO AFFLIATED PRACTICES

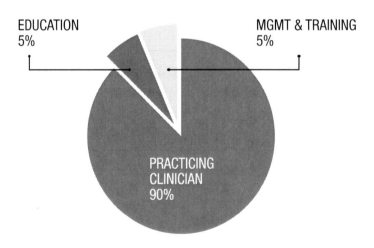

Look how much time is gained for the practitioner when a DSO manages the business-side of the practice.

The DSO Model is All about Freedom

Dov Seidman, founder and chief executive officer of LRN Corporation says:

No organization can ignore that change is underway, any more than a government could ignore the uprising sparked by a Tunisian fruit vendor in 2010. Companies that swim against the tide of history, that invest in more powerful controls and erect walls to keep freedom at bay, will find their smartest minds, most loyal customers, and most valuable partners drift away to seek freedom with others.

Seidman published an article entitled *What Does Freedom in Business Mean to You?* in which he suggests that, "freedom from," in and of itself, is not sufficient; while empowering to individuals, it doesn't establish moral and ethical frameworks in which to operate. "Freedom from" needs to be followed by a meaningful journey toward "freedom to", the shared condition in which we are inspired to act in the common interest. "Freedom to" is an alignment toward shared objectives and mutually positive outcomes.

Those enterprises that devote themselves to fostering "freedom to" will be best suited to generate sustainable growth that is resilient over time. But the only option that can inspire behavior that underpins organizational growth and resilience at the same time is unshackling superfluous controls to foster "freedom from", then embedding and scaling the human values that animate "freedom to."

The DSO Frees the Dentist from:
- Bookkeeping
- Billing
- Lab

- Accounting

- Marketing and advertising

- Information technology

- Human resources

- General office management

- Housekeeping

- Property management

The DSO Frees the Dentist to:

- Create more free time

- Increase quality of patient care

- Increase revenue

- Increase quality of life

- Create professional community

Chapter 14:

Checks and Balances

What better way to learn what is needed in a good and profitable business than to look to a monumental failure in business for some answers? In a paper entitled *Why Many Corporate Compliance and Ethics Programs Are Positioned for Failure*, Donna Boehme and Compliance Strategists, LLC, write about what can be learned from Enron, and its colossal failure. She says:

With the wreckage of the first generation of Enron-type corporate scandals in the rear view mirror, and the chaos of Madoff and the subprime meltdown now all around us, commentators are asking "Where were the ethics officers?" and "Are corporate compliance and ethics programs just window dressing?"

These are fair questions, given that in the years since the 1991 promulgation of the U.S. Organizational Sentencing Guidelines (which set out the roadmap for companies to detect and prevent wrongdoing), several studies have indicated that little progress has been made, and recent events in the corporate world suggest that effective mechanisms to prevent corporate misconduct are lacking.

There is a path forward, moving beyond the sometimes unrealistic assumption of policymakers, boards, and management, on which integrity and compliance can be achieved simply by establishing basic elements such as a formal code of conduct, an ethics officer, a training program, monitoring, and/or an employee helpline, and then expecting that good results will necessarily follow.
In short, we believe that it is time for companies to get serious about corporate culture, accountability, compliance, and ethics, and that the key initial step in achieving this involves the creation of a C-level, empowered compliance and ethics officer: someone with the experience, positioning, mandate, and clout to actually make things happen in the organization.
Compliance helps these groups to avoid becoming an Enron by virtue of using the compliance checklist. Corporations can create environments conducive to the code of ethics. Compliance checklists insure practices are not like the Enron's of the world.

Chapter 15:

On Transforming the Cottage Industry

Necessity is the mother of taking chances. — Mark Twain

Innovation can be the catalyst for growth and success in business, and help you adapt and succeed in the prevailing marketplace. Being innovative does not mean inventing; innovation can mean changing your thinking and your business model by adapting to changes in the environment so as to deliver better products or services. Innovation and transformation go hand in hand.

The DSO model is riding the tide of collective change in business and knows that taking chances to step out in new directions, with an innovative spirit, will ultimately build a stronger dental industry, and create the greatest opportunity for the dentist to succeed.
And sometimes this process of stretching out into the unknown feels like an elephantine task. The following example from India is not what most dentists deal with day to day but it exemplifies our industry if faced with big needs that require large steps of innovation and creative collaboration. The DSO model knows that there is power in both.

Devidasan, a 27-year-old bull elephant from the state of Kerala in India, has had his tooth removed much to his relief. Dentists said they successfully repaired a working elephant's cracked tusk in the first operation of its kind. They performed the procedure on Devidasan by filling the 50 cm (19.6 in) long; 4 cm (1.5 in) deep crack with 47 tubes of a special resin. Amazingly, it appears that Devidasan was not tranquilized during the two-and-a-half-hour operation and he was totally cooperative throughout the procedure.

It was literally an elephantine task, because we had to find specialist equipment and modify it, Dr. Pradeep said. Dr. Pradeep, a professor at the PSM dental college in the town of Trichur, said that if the crack remained untreated, dirt would have gathered inside it and potentially caused a deadly infection. Devidasan's owner was eager to get the operation carried out because the crack in the tusk meant that the animal could not be used in Hindu festivals. Now Devidasan has made a full recovery he has already made his comeback in temple festivals throughout Kerala state.

The seemingly insurmountable problem required a solution and that solution led to innovation and collaboration in order to get the job done.

"Only those who will risk going to far can possibly find out how far they can go".
T. S. Eliot

That Four-Letter Word

The heart of innovation is a four-letter word: Risk. In the innovation
and design section of Bloomberg Business Magazine, Bill Buxton
wrote an article entitled *Why Risk is Important*, all about the importance
of understanding risk as being important to growth and positive change
both in a personal life and in a professional business. In the piece,
Buxton says:

Entrepreneurs, like ice climbers, are often said to risk their necks. But
there are ways to cut danger to sane levels. There are four things that
the prepared ice-climber brings to the base of any climb: training,
tools, fitness, and partners. These tools will help any business or
entrepreneurial endeavor to face risk with confidence and success.

The lessons for business are simple and Buxton's four considerations
employed by the ice climber are exactly the same considerations as
those used by a serial entrepreneur or the effective businessperson
putting forth an innovative business model. "Of course it could
be argued that the rich scope of business constitutes a much more
amorphous challenge than a frozen waterfall," says Buxton. To take a
risk toward possible future success requires four areas you may need to
address:

Training: What, in fact are the skills that would best equip you to
engage your problem? Are they evident on your team? If so, how do
you hone them? If not, how do you bring them onboard?

Tools: What tools are relevant for you to embrace the changing face
of your business or the changing needs of your industry? What are the
potentially useful processes, technologies, or other instruments that
might give you protection throughout this shift?

Fitness: How does one prepare? How rusty are your skills? What
would constitute a warm-up exercise, or a preliminary heat that would

let you find out if you were ready for a new game and a new approach?

Partners: No matter how good you and your team are, in most significant cases you will need partners. Do you have the right ones? Buxton's approach is simple: Get the best. If you can't, you might want to question the wisdom of proceeding.

These four points provide a focus for you as you have the opportunity to flesh out your creativity and address the idea of taking a risk. The more innovation and insight that you bring to determining the answers to each of these four points, and the more effectively you generate the answers, the lower the risk of your endeavor and the higher the probability of exceptional success.

"Fear stifles our thinking and actions. It creates indecisiveness that results in stagnation. I have known talented people who procrastinate indefinitely rather than risk failure. Lost opportunities cause erosion of confidence, and the downward spiral begins."
Charles Stanley

Our Possible Future

"Don't turn away from possible futures until you're certain you don't have anything to learn from them." Richard Bach

More and more dentists are embracing DSOs to help them reduce costs and become more efficient. Through innovative non-clinical support services – including HR, scheduling, IT, accounting, and back-office support – DSOs offer dentists more time to focus on providing quality care to patients at affordable rates. This dental practice structure helps solve both economic and social issues. As a result, we are witnessing the rate of adopting the DSO supported dentistry model now outpacing the traditional practice model.

There is a growing demand from dentists who are looking to maximize their professional potential, yet still have a work/life balance. As a result, there is a significant movement toward larger group practices that are DSO-supported. The ADA Health Policy Resource Center concluded in 2012 that in just two years, the number of large dental group practices had risen 25 percent. This skyrocketing growth suggests that DSOs will represent a more significant sector of dentists in future years. Being both patient-centric and practitioner-centric is at the core of the DSO model. As a result, the future opens opportunity for more patient-centric innovative practice models, especially by utilizing aggregated dental quality and patient satisfaction analytics. The DSO model also supports the dentist in their ongoing education and development through mentorships with successful, experienced dentists and by providing advanced leadership and clinical training programs. These are already part of many of the present DSO models.

The DSO community is growing and adapting to a changing environment with clarity and creative collaboration. Like any other movement, it's not perfect, but the industry is learning and maturing.

It is said that the world reserves its more amazing rewards for the courageous and the bold and for those with the courage to pursue their dreams with confidence and an open mind and heart. Our changing times will call for the courageous to step forward and will ultimately see others fall to the side. Where will you choose to stand? Our cottage industry is transforming – let's embrace it.

"You've got to jump off cliffs all the time and build your wings on the way down."
Annie Dillard

The opinions and information included in "Transforming the Cottage Industry" are those put forth by Dr. Quinn Dufurrena the author.

Any and all proceeds of this book will go to the Dentists for Oral Health Innovation.

Dr. Barreto is not a spokesperson for Perfect Teeth and the opinions reflected in this interview are her own opinions and not necessarily the opinions of Perfect Teeth.

Quinn Dufurrena, DDS, JD
19751 E. Mainstreet, Suite #340
Parker, Colorado 80138
qdufurrena@theadso.org
www.TheADSO.org